Running a
Stables as a
Business

Running a Stables as a Business

JANET W MACDONALD

J. A. Allen
London

© Janet W. Macdonald 1980 and 1998
First published in Great Britain 1980
Revised edition 1998
Reprinted 2006
Reprinted 2008

ISBN 978 0 85131 737 3

J.A. Allen
Clerkenwell House
Clerkenwell Green
London EC1R 0HT

J.A. Allen is an imprint of Robert Hale Limited

www.halebooks.com

Design by Judy Linard
Printed in China
and arranged by New Era Printing Co. Limited, Hong Kong

Contents

Acknowledgements

My grateful thanks to all the people who helped me by providing information for this book: the Association of British Riding Schools; Mrs Joyce Bellamy of Thornton Heath for information on rates and planning permission; the staff of Midland Bank plc (West Wickham branch); Philip Murphy for information on accounting and taxation; the late Mr Norman Simmons for information on indoor schools; South Essex Insurance Brokers; Mrs Joan Kinney for information on the American scene; all my stable-owning friends who tolerated my impertinent questions; *Light Horse* (now *Horse and Rider*) magazine, where much of the original version of this book first appeared in a series of articles, and last but by no means least my husband, Ken Maxwell-Jones, for information on life assurance and investments – and regular supplies of coffee!

Introduction

When I wrote the first version of this book in 1980, I stated in
the introduction that eight out of ten riding schools and livery
yards in the UK seemed to be badly run, with tatty premises
and barely adequate standards of horse care. That situation
has, thankfully, changed, but there are still some tatty establishments out there.

No stable owner deliberately sets out to run a shabby establishment, and most only accept the situation they are in
because familiarity has dulled their critical senses. So how
does it happen? I am convinced that it is because the people
who run these yards not only have no basic business training,
but are firmly convinced that they do not need it. They think
the prime requisite for running a stables is to know all about
horses, and that knowing about management and accountancy is of no importance whatsoever.

They do not even understand that what they are running is
a *business*, and that the basic principles of running any business are the same, regardless of whether that business is selling horse-care or nuts and bolts. Business is about MONEY,
and it is the lack of money that makes these places so tatty.

If you don't have enough money coming in, or you are
wasting what does come in, the only way you can retain
enough to live on is to skimp on the horses' feed, or on fixing
the stable roofs. If there isn't enough spare cash to pay wages,
you will have to do all the work yourself, and you will soon get
too tired to do it properly, or even to care if it is done properly.

So, to run your business properly, you *must* think about

money. No one expects you to think about it all the time, but you should be aware of its importance and plan ahead to utilise what does come your way to your own best advantage. You should know exactly what everything costs and what it can earn, and ruthlessly weed out the non-earners and money-wasters, or to use a naval phrase, 'run a tight ship'.

The purpose of this book is to show established stable owners how to run a 'tighter ship', and to suggest ways of maximising opportunities, and also to provide all the basic information the prospective stable owner needs. I have tried to keep it readable and friendly, rather than dwelling too much on the fine details of legalities and staff management, which have been dealt with in far more detail in the 'sister' volume, *The Horse: Equestrian Business* (Julie Brega, J.A. Allen).

Please note that my use of the feminine gender when referring to customers, staff and proprietors is a reflection of the higher numbers of females than males involved with horses, and does not imply any sexist motive on my part. To redress the balance, I've referred to professionals (lawyers, accountants, etc.) in the masculine, although we all know that a significant proportion are female.

1
Finding and Financing the Right Place

Once you are sure that you really do want to make your living by running a stables, you must then find a stables to run. You may find an existing business for sale, or some empty premises that you can develop, but almost certainly you will have definite ideas on the type of yard you want, and this will influence the areas that will suit your purposes.

Geographical Location

To a certain extent, the geographical location will depend on your intended usage. Show yards, studs, and rehabilitation or quarantine centres do not need regular access by customers, and can therefore be fairly remote. Trekking and holiday centres will have to be located in attractive countryside, but can also be remote, since each customer will come only once or twice a year. The usual practice in this situation is to provide transport to and from the nearest station each week for any customers who do not want to travel by car.

Livery stables and riding schools must be within easy reach of the paying customers, who will not come on the regular basis you want if you are too far away or too difficult to reach. However, most livery owners will have their own transport, so for them it will not matter too much if you are several miles off a main road – all the better, perhaps, from the hacking point of view.

Riding schools, especially those catering for children, may

benefit from being close to a bus route, as some of your pupils will not have a parent to fetch them to and fro in a car. To provide a steady flow of customers, a good catchment area is needed. The better class of housing estates will provide a steady source of revenue, and local schools and colleges may provide customers to ride in your 'off-peak' weekday hours.

Local Knowledge

It is always easier to set up business in an area where you know the local conditions, and where you yourself are known. This latter point is especially valuable where the bank is concerned – but more of that later. Often the local grapevine will tell you that a suitable yard is about to become available before it is advertised; and as often as not it is the availability of such a place that propels the ambition to have your own yard from the back to the forefront of your mind. 'I could do a good job of running that place', you think.

Once you have somewhere specific in mind, you will need to go and have a look at it, and perhaps ask some questions of the locals which will help you in your decision. The first thing you need to know is whether the yard has a poor reputation. This could be for low standards of horse-care and tuition, general nuisance value to local residents, or non-payment of bills, and you do not want to find that you have been tarred with the same brush of ill-feeling. Although you can notify suppliers of the change of ownership, and place adverts in the local papers to let other people know, it can take years before the legacy wears off.

Background to the Business

There are a lot of questions that you must ask about the background to any business.

The most common motive for hanging out the For Sale sign is that business is bad, so the first, and most important question is: 'Why is this place available?' The next should be: 'How many people have had it in the last ten years?' If the answer to the second question is more than two, you have the answer to the first at hand; for some reason, it is not profitable, and you would be wise to forget it. Are you really so talented that you can make a go of a business where others have failed?

There are, of course, other reasons for a yard being available that may make you decide against it, such as an imminent motorway through the middle of it, and such aspects should be carefully checked. This is something that other local businesses may know about.

It is rare to find a stables offered as a going concern but, if this is the case, there is a separate set of questions to ask. Do the seller's claims about the business tally with his or her actual accounts and tax returns? Is the price asked fair and reasonable? For instance, what value has been placed on the goodwill? Are there any outstanding bills for you to pay? These could include rates and taxes, or wages/redundancy costs of any staff who are departing at the changeover. Are there any outstanding payments to the business for you to collect, and how likely are you to be paid? (Such payments might include fees for block lessons from a local school or charity for disabled riders.) Does the inventory tally with the items actually to be seen, and is the seller prepared to make proper arrangements to ensure that all is handed over? Is there anything that you will have to dispose of at a loss, like awful riding school horses, or awful tack, or can you refuse to accept these as part of the bargain?

Why the anxiety to sell? Here is the 'motorway' type of problem again, or maybe the bank is about to foreclose on the mortgage. And finally, does the seller actually own what is being offered to you? This last point should always be checked by a solicitor. Often the explanation given for the sale is that the proprietor wants to retire, or has some other family-related reason to sell. Don't let the plausibility of such reasons prevent you from making all the usual checks.

Next, how long can you have the yard for? Unless you are intending to buy the freehold, you must check the length of the lease left and its renewability, or the terms of renting. There is no point in putting a lot of effort into a yard that you will have to vacate within a few years, before starting the long and expensive process of finding somewhere else!

The next question is perhaps the most crucial, and it is failure to find the answer to it that has caused the bankruptcy of many inexperienced business people. How much will the yard cost to run? If you are buying, and borrowing the money, you must take the interest into account. If the property is in need of running repairs, you must take the cost of these into account. Finally you must check the overheads, rates, insurance, etc. Business rates are a particularly important consideration. They can be very high, and it will do nasty things to your profit margin if you have to compete with somebody over the borough border whose rates are less.

If the answers to these questions are satisfactory, there are some more specific points to be considered. What is the local competition? Do you really want to spend all your time poaching their customers, or vice versa? Are the management standards of the competition so low that there is a risk of infection at times of epidemics? (Equine influenza, metritis, etc.) Will you share the blame for their misdemeanours? Will their reaction to your higher standards be ill-will, or even sabotage?

Are there any other undesirable close neighbours, such as airfields, noisy factories or nasty housing estates full of vandals, all ready to frighten the horses?

Existing Amenities

If the premises are not already being used for your intended purpose, will the local council allow you to use them for that purpose? Is there living accommodation for yourself and your staff, or will you be allowed to use a caravan?

What are the local weather conditions? Is this the one spot for miles around that disappears under a low cloud every time it rains, or becomes impassable every time it snows?

Do the fields have good soil and drainage, or sticky clay,

impossible to ride in after rain and baked hard in the summer? Is the land in good heart, or are you going to have to spend a lot of money on restoring it? Is the actual grazing usable immediately, free of weeds or poisonous plants, or rubbish to hurt the horses, and with good fences and gates? Is there an adequate method of getting water to the fields, and easy access for tractors? How accessible is it generally, to customers, horseboxes, delivery lorries and such other useful visitors as the cess-pit emptier and the dustcart?

Does it have everything else in the way of amenities that you want, or a place where they can be provided? Easy access to hacking, without recourse to main roads, is almost essential; a manège, or space for one, with an adequate electricity supply *is* essential these days. Gates big enough for horseboxes are nice, loos are even nicer, and there are many other items you may feel you would like to have if possible

Are the buildings going to need repair, renovation or alteration before they are usable? Are all the fittings such as hay racks there, or are you going to have to buy them? Does the water system work in all weathers? Is there adequate storage space for hard feed, hay and bedding, and somewhere to store manure?

Raising Finance

All these questions centre upon the most important point: can you afford to buy this place, and can you make a profit out of it? If the overall answer is 'No', or only 'Maybe', then perhaps you should look for somewhere else.

If, after all this, you decide you do want the place, it is time to think of money. For straightforward renting this is a minor point, although you should keep in mind that your income from the yard may be low for a while, and you should have enough saved to pay the rent for at least six months. Do get a solicitor to check the terms of the tenancy, to be sure they allow you to do all the things you want to do. They may not allow you to sub-let, for instance, and letting someone else have boxes for their own use may bring in some welcome cash when you are short. You should also be sure for how long you have to pay the rent. It may be a fixed term of a year, regardless of whether or not you are using the premises, and you may have to pay several months rent at the beginning of the tenancy. There may also be some form of 'key' payment to be made.

If a lease, or the freehold, must be purchased, and you do not have the cash handy, or a kind uncle whom you can tap for a loan, you will have to go to a commercial institution to ask for a loan. Prices vary tremendously according to location, facilities, and many other factors, but there is no doubt that you will have to find a substantial sum of money. One problem is that no bank or other source of finance will lend you the whole amount. You will be expected to put up at least a third yourself, and possibly half. Banks call this your 'venture capital', and while this is comparatively easy to find through venture capital brokers in the USA, where the tax laws are kinder, in the UK it is extremely difficult for this sort of business. Consider the percentage return that a stables is going to bring, compare that with the likely return of any other sort of business, and you will soon see why no one who has to pay full tax is going to be interested in your idea. So, if you don't have a big chunk of venture capital in the bank before you start, forget buying, and find a place you can rent.

There is a possibility, in rural areas, that you may be able to obtain a grant. The best source of information and assistance in drawing up the grant application is either the regional office of the Agricultural Development and Advisory Service (ADAS) or the Rural Development Commission (formerly CoSIRA). In some cases, the Ministry of Agriculture, Fisheries and Food (MAFF) will give grants to full-time farmers who are seeking to diversify, so you might think of starting your stable in partnership with a farmer.

Ordinary building societies will not provide money for business loans, but the Agricultural Mortgage Corporation might. Ask ADAS to help you investigate this. Otherwise, you will have to go to a bank or finance house, and they will need quite a lot of convincing before they will let you have the money.

Their first concern will be with you personally, and your past financial history. This is where it helps to go to a bank that knows you. If your history is steady and sensible – no unauthorised overdrafts, no living hand to mouth or other signs of inability to handle money – they will then consider you as a business person. They will ask whether you have ever run this sort of business or any other before, and if so, how successfully? They will also ask whether you have any qualifications. However, a history of running any sort of business, even if it had nothing to do with horses, will impress potential lenders far more than qualifications relating to horses. If you have a close relative with business experience it will help if you set your business up as a limited company, with that experienced person as one of the directors.

Next, the bank will consider the business itself. Is it to be a new venture, or are you taking over an existing one? Has it been consistently profitable? They will want proof of this, in the form of copies of the audited accounts for several years. They will also want to know what the premises are like, whether you have had them valued and whether you have plans and estimates for any improvements.

What all this boils down to is that they want to be satisfied that you can make a success of the venture, and repay them regularly without causing them any trouble. Once they are convinced of this, they will want some security on the loan, and in these circumstances this is most likely to take the form of a first charge on the property, and assignment of the 'goodwill'. They will also require you to insure the property in a form acceptable to them, and may very well want you to insure your own life for the total amount of the loan.

Finally the period of the loan, interest rate and repayment periods will be set. The period of loans for property purposes can be up to twenty-five years. Repayments will probably be at six-monthly intervals to a bank, and monthly intervals to a finance house.

Not all finance house are prepared to make small business

loans, so you may have to look around for the right one. If you do discover one, you will find that their interest rates will be at least 1.5 per cent higher than a bank's, so on the whole you are probably better off going to a bank anyway.

Start with your own bank. If they won't lend you the money, ask why not. If the answer is the lame excuse that you want a sum over the manager's limit, or that he has lent his quota for the year, or if he is honest enough to tell you that he doesn't fancy the proposition, you are then at liberty to go to another bank that does. In which case, you will be expected to move all you banking business across.

At this point, rather than start yourself on the long traipse around all the local banks and finance houses, you would do better to enlist the help of a financial expert who does this work all the time. By this I mean one of those much-maligned people – a life assurance salesman. Don't shy away from the idea – wherever you borrow money, you will have to insure your life as part of the loan agreement. The life salesman's reward for doing the leg-work in finding you the money you need is the commission he earns on the life policy. Furthermore you can and should leave the work to him. You'll only muddy the waters if you try as well. His local contacts will know that he won't offer them a poor proposition, and the fact that he presents yours to them is a point in its favour. He will start with his local contacts and move further afield if necessary; he may well know of a bank manager in some other part of the country who is amenable to such cases.

Some insurance brokers specialise in this type of business, as do many 'tied' agents. The latter work for the big unit-linked life assurance companies. Find the companies from their advertisements in the Sunday papers; find their local office in the phone book and ask for an appointment with one of their senior agents who specialise in small business loans.

Interest rates in these matters are arranged as follows. There exists a thing called base rate. This is either finance house base rate, or bank base rate (sometimes called minimum lending rate). This goes up and down according to the state of the economy, or the government's budget requirements. For the type of loan in question, you will have to pay from 2 to 6 per cent over base, so if the bank rate is 6 per cent, you would be paying from 8 per cent to 12 per cent; if bank rate is 10 per cent, you will be paying 12 per cent to 16 per cent. This does not mean that you will be paying the same rate of interest for the whole period of the loan, set when you take it out, but that as the bank rate fluctuates, so will your rate of interest.

However, as you will probably be repaying the principal (capital sum) as you go, the amount of interest will become less as time goes by. Interest is calculated daily, on the amount of the principal outstanding, so if you should find yourself with some money to spare, it might be worth considering making an extra payment against the principal.

Once your loan is approved, the finance house gives you a cheque, or the bank opens a loan account for you, and transfers the money to your current account and you are in business. Either institution will be happier if you sign a standing order for the repayments, and woe betide you if that money is not available on time. Two weeks late and they will start writing rude letters – a few more weeks, and they will get your deeds out of the vaults and start looking at them with an acquisitive gleam in their eyes!

2

Money Matters

An argument one often encounters from stable proprietors on the subject of costing and charging is 'If we did it the way our accountant wants us to, we'd have to charge so much that all our clients would go'. This may be taking the issue to an extreme, but it does point up the fact that many stables are run by horse people, not business people; and that the concept of a horse business, as seen by the two parties, is wellnigh incompatible. The horse person considers that expertise in horse-care is the prime consideration, and that money matters come a poor second, so long as they manage to eat regularly. The business person considers that the prime objective should be to make a profit, and that the sums must be done properly to ensure that this is the case. They also think that the owner of a business should have business skills before technical skills, which, whether those of an electronics expert or a horse expert, can be employed fairly easily. Obviously, where a small business is concerned, to employ these skills eats away the profit, but the principle is still the same.

Accountants, Costings and Profit Margins

The average business operates at pre-tax profits of at least 25 per cent. To the accountant who is used to this, the concept of a business proprietor who is prepared to run at a profit margin of under 5 per cent, as is often the case with stables, is difficult to reconcile with his normal experience. To a certain extent, it could be said that your willingness to operate your business at such a low profit margin is none of your accountant's business, but it *is* his business to warn you of impending disaster. After all, if you do go bankrupt, he may not get paid!

Much of the problem lies in the accountant's use of jargon. To him, debits, credits, arrears and budgeting are the stuff of his everyday life. To the lay person, they are mystic symbols of how complex accountancy is, and such people often just close their mind to the whole thing.

The danger in the scornful attitude of some stable owners to the accountant's point of view is that they are likely to ignore his warnings and fail to do their costings at regular intervals. And, worse yet, fail to adjust their charges accordingly. Costs creep up a little here, a little there, and although you may moan when the price of oats goes up yet again, if you do not take this into account when setting your fees, you may not realise that you are eroding your profit margin until it is too late.

While it is easy enough to cost the food and bedding each horse uses, it is not so obvious to the beginner that overheads and depreciation should also be costed. Overheads are all those expenses which occur regardless of whether or not there are any horses in the yard – electricity, wages, rates, etc. Depreciation is the accountant's word to describe the fact that fixed assets (buildings, for example), will eventually fall down and be worth nothing. This means they will have to be replaced, and so they are charged for over a fixed term, to allow finances to be available for replacement when needed. If a loose box costs £2,000 to build, and lasts ten years, then you should depreciate it at £200 a year. And the person who is using it should be charged for that depreciation. Depreciation should not be confused with maintenance, which is the cost of keeping the asset in good working order.

So, when you fix your charges, you should first add up all your overheads, then add depreciation, and divide that by the number of boxes in the yard, and again by twelve to obtain a monthly cost. Then, to that figure, add the cost of food and bedding for each horse, and you have the true monthly cost of keeping each horse. Then add a bit more for your profit, and you will be running a business, not subsidising your clients' hobby out of your own pocket!

Calculating one's profit margin is a matter of balancing a proper profit against what the market will bear. A sensible person does her sums every six months, and makes small increases to her charges in a way which upsets no one too much. A £20 increase on a monthly livery bill twice a year hurts no one, but a £200 increase after five years at the same price is rather painful. It might even lose you some indignant clients, and it has certainly lost you a lot of money over the five years – £5,400 per livery to be precise. Multiply that by the number of boxes in your yard, and you'll begin to see what your accountant is on about!

I'm assuming that you are planning to use an accountant. Nobody, unless experienced in the work themselves, should be rash enough to try to operate a business without one, especially now the dreaded 'self-assessment' is with us. Not only do accountants know all about taxes, and provide an experienced buffer between you and the Inland Revenue; they will also perform a multitude of other services. They will do your book-keeping, work out salaries and PAYE, do your VAT returns, and almost anything else you can think of. But do remember that they charge on time spent, so expecting them to work from scrappy pieces of paper, having to telephone you to clarify details and other time-wasting trivia, is going to cost you extra.

As a general guide, it is a good idea to choose an affluent accountant. If he can't handle his own financial affairs properly, he won't do much for yours. In addition to doing straight-forward accounting work the one you want is going to suggest to you how you can save tax, rather than waiting until you ask him how to do it.

How do you find the paragon you need? Ideally by personal recommendation from someone who is in the same line of business as yourself which, in this context, includes farmers. If that fails, ask your bank manager to recommend one. Indeed, most banks have a department of their own which does this sort of thing, but do remember that if you are running a limited company, your accounts must be audited by a firm of Chartered Accountants.

Here I've made another basic assumption – that you are intending to have at least one bank account. Some people think that doing without one and making all their transactions in cash will prevent the Inland Revenue and other nosy people from knowing what they are doing. This is not true – the average taxman wasn't born yesterday, and he is more likely to be suspicious in these circumstances.

Using Your Bank

If you have a bank account, you can pay your bills more easily (unless your suppliers distrust you so much that they insist on cash!) by putting a cheque in the post instead of having to keep large sums of money handy. Furthermore, there are other advantages in having a bank account. Consider this example: if you buy your hay when it is made, and collect it from the field yourself, it is very cheap. If you buy it from a feed merchant or farmer in small amounts during the year, the cost is higher, and it gets higher still as the year progresses. By the New Year, you can be paying double the original price. But, if you have a bank account, and you are on good terms with your bank manager, he will let you have an overdraft at haymaking time, and you can buy all your hay at the cheapest price. But what about the overdraft interest, you'll be asking. Well, let's assume that you need fifty tons of hay to get you through the year, and that in June it costs £150 per ton. Fifty tons will cost £7,500. If the interest on that is 20 per cent (which is very high, and not likely unless the base rate is over 16 per cent), paying back £1000 a month, on a reducing balance over nine months, the interest will be £580, so your year's supply of hay will have cost you £8,080. If hay starts out at £150 in June, and increases by £30 per ton every two months, by the end of March it will be costing £270. If you buy ten tons every two months, by the end of the year, your fifty tons of hay will have cost you £10,500, which is £2,420 more than doing it the overdraft way.

What I am trying to point out here is not merely the advantage of being able to use the bank's money as well as your own, but the necessity, in these inflationary times, for you to develop a fiscal awareness, and look further than the end of your nose. Far too many of the stable proprietors I have met seem to live for today instead of planning ahead, and do the silliest things, like selling a horse when they have a big bill to pay, instead of going to their bank manager for help.

Another common fault, incidentally, is a stubborn refusal to accept losses. The wise businessperson accepts that some losses are inevitable, and has the wit to minimise them by accepting them, and keeping them small by immediate action. For instance, if you have a horse who you hope to sell for a profit, and it becomes obvious that you are not going to be able to do so, then get rid of him quick, at the best price you can. Taking £500 less than you would like is better than spending £1,000 in keeping him for another two months in order to get your fixed price. Keeping him that length of time is not only going to cost money, it also means that the horse's value is tied up in that horse, instead of being available for you to use in some other way. If you must keep items in the hope of selling them, at least keep those that do not eat anything!

Basic Security

After which digression, back to cash – the folding variety. Your insurance company, as well as common sense, will require you to consider security arrangements. A lockable cash box is essential, a safe for larger amounts is advisable, and so are regular trips to the bank and even night safe facilities for weekends. This applies especially to riding schools, where weekends are busy, and payments for lessons will mostly be in cash. (And if you are thinking that this has advantageous possibilities, remember that your accountant and possibly the taxman and VAT inspector will want to see your lesson bookings, to tie them up with your takings.)

All this talk about safes may sound a bit excessive, but it is only common sense, as is the necessity for an awareness of how much cash you should have at any given time. I still remember with horror the busy riding school where I used to keep my horse at livery. The cash box used to stand, unlocked, in the proprietor's kitchen, which was frequented by all the working pupils and many of the clients. Most of these people had doubtless seen, as I had, the proprietor open the cash box, take out a handful of money and put it into her purse, *without counting it*, when she wanted to go shopping. In other words, practically everybody knew that she did not know how much money there should be in that cash box, and therefore would not know if anyone was helping themselves to some. It is perhaps relevant to mention that this establishment was soon sold, as this lady's careless attitude to money and allied matters caught up with her, and she got into financial difficulties.

Outstanding Debts

Another of this lady's problems stemmed from the fact that she didn't like anything unpleasant, and never did anything about livery clients who didn't pay their bills. I will discuss this specific aspect in Chapter 9 – Liveries, but debt collection is another aspect of any business which does not deal solely in instant cash, and it is something you should be aware of.

If you have outstanding accounts, and the people who owe you money are no longer regularly on your premises, you should first send them a copy invoice, then a statement, with a 'this seems to have escaped your attention' letter. If this fails, you write an 'or else' letter, and if that fails, you get your solicitor to do the same. This is usually enough to frighten the offender into paying, but if they still do not, here are your options:

• Write it down to experience and forget it. This is the best bet if the amount is less than £250, as it could easily cost you that much to recover it. But don't weep too much, bad debts are tax-deductible.

- Instruct your solicitor to go ahead and sue, as he will have threatened in his rude letter. But beware, if the debt is small,* even if the court finds in your favour, you will not be awarded costs, and you will have to pay your solicitor's fees yourself. Still, legal fees are tax-deductible, too.
- Do without a solicitor and institute proceedings yourself, at the local County Court. Ask the Registrar's department for the booklet on Small Claims. You will find the staff very helpful, but they are not allowed to give you legal advice, so word your questions carefully.
- Find a debt collection agency. They are not likely to be interested in small amounts either, and they will require either a fee, or a percentage of what they recover, for their trouble.
- Get a couple of large men, and go knocking on the offender's door. But I jest – this is illegal, and they might call the police. Or find a couple of large friends of their own, and come and see you late one night. . .

* currently £5,000 or less, but this figure may be subject to change

3
Cash Books and Cash Flows

Whatever you give your accountant at the end of the year in the way of accounts-producing material, you must keep day-to-day records yourself. Remember that VAT officials may call and demand to see your records, and woe betide you if they are more than a month behind.

Keeping Records

The simplest form of cash book is one where you just list everything, without attempting to analyse it. Get a ruled book from the stationers, use the left hand side of each double page for income and the right hand side for outgoings. This is the way every other business does it, so don't confuse your accountant's staff by being different. Make a note each day of how much you have paid into the bank, and how much you have drawn out of the bank, as well as cash that passes through your hands. Keep all invoices and receipts.

This job should take you less than an hour each week, and it is the minimum you must do. It is going to take your accountant a long time to unravel it, and check it against your bank statements, and he will charge you accordingly. It is a method which does not give you much information, either, such as whether your lesson income is increasing or decreasing over the months.

The other way to keep books is only a little more time-consuming for you, but saves your accountant hours of tedious (and, to you, expensive) work. It also provides you with at-a-glance information on your financial affairs. For this, you will need a little more in the way of books. You will need one book for cash (called the petty cash book) and one for bank transactions (this one is called the cash book – confusing, isn't it?). Both will need to be ruled in cash columns, with a wide column on the left for details and dates. The petty cash book needn't be large, as it will need only about six columns per page, but the cash book will need about six columns for income, and about ten for expenditure.

For the cash book, start a new page each month and head up the columns for the items you receive regularly and spend on regularly – but keep the first two columns of income and the first one of expenses for basic bank details. On the income side, the first column should be for incoming amounts as they occur. Put the name of the person who gave you the cheque or cash in the details column and the amount in the next column, then, if the whole amount was for one thing, for example livery, put that amount again in its own column. If the cheque was for more than one thing, say, livery and lessons, or *if it includes VAT*, split it into its component parts and enter it accordingly.

When you want to pay some money into the bank, draw a line under the last entry in the first column, add the amounts, and put the total in the second column, alongside that line. This amount should tally with the total on the paying-in slip, which will make it much easier to check off bank statements. Checking is further simplified if you enter details on the back of the paying-in stub in the same order as those in the cash book.

For expenditure, it is just as easy. When you write a cheque, fill in the stub with the date and amount of money, the name of the person you paid and the item you paid for – and, if VAT was involved, the amount of that. (For example: 12th July. F.Bloggs. Farrier. Two horses. VAT £14.00, Total £94.00.) Then all you have to do at cash book time is put down the name, date and cheque number (so it can be checked off against the bank statement), write the amount of the cheque in the first column, and allocate the amount as before in its respective columns.

For both income and expenses, there will be items that crop up occasionally, but not often enough to have a column of their own – like manure sales, or the three-monthly payment of VAT. For recording such items you have a column marked 'Other', with a space next to it where you can note precisely what it was.

For the petty cash book, you do not need cheque numbers or banking details, but otherwise the method is the same. When you want to bank some cash, you make an entry on the expenditure side 'banked £xxxx' and put it on the income side of the cash book as 'petty cash'. If you get money from the bank, you enter it in the cash book like any other cheque, and in the petty cash book as 'income from bank, cheque no. 123'.

Doing things this way will take an hour a week, and also another hour at the end of the month, when you add up all the columns and put the invoices in order. Put a paper-clip on each month's collection, and put them away safely. With these columns added, not only can you see how you are doing, but your VAT return will be easier, and you will have the figures handy for your cash flow.

To Recap:
- Use left hand side of book for income, right hand side for expenditure.
- Fill in cheque stubs properly.
- Fill in paying-in stubs properly.
- Start a new pair of pages for each month.
- Add up each column at the end of the month.

And the golden rules:
- Note cash income and expenditure daily.
- Write up your cash books every week, while you can still remember any items you didn't make a note of.
- Make sure you get, and keep, receipts for *all* business expenditure.

Examples of both cash and petty cash books are shown in Appendices 1 and 2.

Budgeting

One task your accountant will press you about is budgeting, which is a fancy term to describe the simple fact that you should be prepared to meet certain expenses at regular intervals, and must have the money available. Consider the implications: many of your expenses, such as wages, feed or shoeing bills will have to be paid every week or month, but others, such as telephone, rates, or loan interest are only due at three- or even six-monthly intervals. It is sensible to set a little aside each month in preparation for these payments, and even more sensible to make these small sums earn a little more for you while they are waiting. Even building society interest is better than nothing, and there are short-term investments which will bring in a little more. Ask your bank manager – and absorb the concept that money will breed more money if you treat it right. Keeping cash under your bed does not give it a chance to breed.

Even if most of the money that comes in is in the form of cheques, you should get it into the bank as soon as you can. If it isn't in the bank, it is neither earning you interest nor reducing your overdraft and thus saving interest. Unless it is a small amount, or you have a long drive to the bank (and have to pay to park) you should aim to get all money into the bank within 24 hours.

Budgeting is a task which causes even the most experienced business people to quake in their shoes, which is silly. Like many jobs that you put off doing because you think that they are going to be awful, when you actually get down to it, budgeting is easy, and quick to do. In your case it is easier than many other businesses, for you can pinpoint pretty accurately what your expenses and income will be. Each livery costs so much and earns so much; each school horse costs so much and earns so much. You have a specific number of boxes in your yard, and a specific amount of grazing. If you intend to build more boxes, you know how much they will cost – and so on and so on. All you have to do is build up this information into an easily readable form. Accountants call this a cash flow forecast, and it really is easy to do. An example of a cash flow forecast is shown in Appendix 3, and it is produced in the following way.

Get two large sheets of ruled and columned paper – you will need one wide column on the left for details, and eighteen small ones for figures. On the first sheet, taking two columns per month, head up the first twelve columns for the next six months of the year. The next four columns will be for the last two quarters of the year, and the final two for totals. You should now have pairs of columns marked January, February, March, April, May, June, July to September, October to December, Total. Head up the second sheet in quarter years and totals, and that gives you the next two years. Finally, mark each pair of columns 'Actual' and 'Budget'.

Now for the details. Use the top half of the page for income and the bottom half for expenses. Allow a line in the middle for totals, and three lines at the bottom for totals, balances and cumulative balances. Allowing one line for each item, fill in all the items you receive (livery, lessons, sales, bank interest, etc.) and all you spend (rates and rent, loan repayments, feed, wages, etc.) and make sure you have one marked 'Contingencies'. This is to allow for all the disasters that can hit you when you least expect them. If you allow some money to deal with them, they won't hurt so much. Don't forget to include your own wages when it comes to expenses!

Having done that, you can begin to put in some figures. Work out how much each item earns/costs each month , and fill in the budget columns. Don't forget to multiply by three for the 'Quarters' columns, and don't forget seasonal variation, like bad weather in January/February, which will reduce your income from lessons and probably increase your costs. This will be easy for the first period of six months, as you can be fairly sure what things will cost, but you must make allowances for inflation further ahead. I would suggest a ten per cent increase every six months.

Having done all this (and you must make allowances for *everything*), you can then add up the columns. First, total the income and expenses, then deduct expenses from income and put the result in the balance line. If expenses are more than income, and you get a minus figure, put brackets around it (this is an accounting convention to indicate a minus figure). Now you can do the cumulative balances. Just add the month's balance to the previous month's cumulative balance. Hopefully this will increase steadily as the months progress, but it may go into negative figures at times.

You now have an advanced picture of the development or decline of your business. It may scare the living daylights out of you, but it will tell you the truth about your chances of success or bankruptcy. It will prepare you for the lean months, so that you have cash ready, instead of that panic to sell something below its true value to pay the bills. It will tell you when you will be able to afford those new boxes, or if you can afford the repayments on a loan to build the indoor school you desperately need. It will also convince your bank manager not only that you can afford those repayments, but that you are a responsible business person instead of a reckless fool, blundering blindly along in the dark, hoping everything will turn out right.

One final point on these cash flow forecasts: the more you do them, the better your guesstimates of amounts will become, and this is where those 'Actual' columns come in. Every month, when you add up the columns in your cash books, fill in this column on your cash flow. Then you can compare 'Actual' with 'Budget', see how accurate your guesstimates were – and prove that accuracy to your bank manager.

4
Profits, Losses and the Taxman

Everyone knows what a profit is. It is the gain you make when you sell something for more than it has cost you. If you sell something for less than it cost, then the result is a loss, not a profit. But there is a snag, as always. The profit just described is called a gross profit, and it is subject to tax. When the taxman has had his bit, what is left is called net profit, and that is what you have to live on. So obviously, the less the taxman gets, the more you get, and we come back to the point I keep labouring – that a good accountant is worth his weight in gold, for his tax know-how will save you much more than his fee.

Taxation

Taxation is a complex field, and since each National Budget tends to change the situation, the help of an expert to maximise opportunities is essential. All you have to understand is the difference between tax evasion and tax avoidance. Evasion is illegal and dishonest, as it involves deliberately taking action to evade paying tax that is lawfully due. Avoidance is perfectly legal, and it hinges on a famous court decision which said that there is no legal bar to arranging one's financial affairs in such a way as to reduce one's tax liabilities to a minimum.

The main area in which a small business can reduce its tax liability is by ensuring that all legitimate expenses have been claimed. A legitimate expense is one that relates to the running of the business. Coffee for the proprietor's home use does not, but coffee for the staff's morning break does, as do the chairs they sit on while they drink it. Dog food might be a legitimate expense, but not if you live a long way from the stables and take the dog home with you. There is no laid down rule as to the type of dog concerned, the principle here is that it is a guard dog, which means that it must be on the premises it is meant to be guarding. You can, however, take it to horse shows with you, for then it will be guarding your horsebox.

A proportion of the expenses of your own personal horse could even be deductible if you are using him in the business. How are you going to do that in a livery stable? Well, if you have working pupils, you need a horse for them to practise such skills as plaiting and clipping, for you cannot let them loose with clippers on clients' horses, and so you will need a horse to teach them on. Just be ready to substantiate this use to the taxman, for it is on such points that he is inclined to be sticky.

What all this boils down to is that you must keep a note of *all* expenditure (and the receipts) and let your accountant decide what is legitimately claimable. If you are considering any radical changes in your field of operation, buying any expensive equipment, or even changing your car, consult him first. It might be advantageous to time these moves according to your year end, the last budget, or just your general situation. Trust your accountant, and let him utilise the fiscal skills you are paying for, to your best advantage.

Limited Companies and Sole Traders

I mentioned limited companies in Chapter 2, and you may want to consider starting one for your business. Whether or not this is a good idea depends in the final analysis on your individual circumstances, and you must discuss these with your accountant but, as always, there are pros and cons.

First, it costs more to start a limited company than to set up trading on your own account (called 'sole trader') or as a partnership. Stamp duties must be paid, certain statutory books must be purchased, and so must a company seal. The usual procedure is for your accountant to purchase a ready-made company, complete with everything needed, from a firm which specialises in starting companies. This will cost about £100. All you have to do is fill in the forms showing your shareholders and directors and send them to the Registrar of Companies. (To commence trading as a sole trader or partnership, you don't have to do anything formal and there is no longer a requirement to register business names.)

Next, a limited company has to submit a list of shareholders, directors and other details, called an annual return, complete with a copy of the audited accounts, to the Registrar of Companies every year. You must pay a small fee each year for the privilege of having these documents filed at Companies House, where anybody can go along and look at them to see what you are doing. Sole traders and partnerships do not have to file such information, and you may prefer to maintain your privacy.

Limited companies are subject to corporation tax on their profits before dividends are paid – which effectively means you will be taxed twice, as you will also have to pay income tax on the dividends when you receive them. This last point may be purely academic, as you will probably be drawing all the profit as director's salary or paying into your pension fund (of which more in Chapter 6).

There are also certain legal restrictions on exactly what you may or may not do with a limited company and its money, which do not arise with a sole trader or partnership. All this may seem to add up to a lot of points against having a limited company. However, they are all offset by the great advantage of having limited liability. If you are a sole trader, and your business fails, your creditors can make you bankrupt, and that means you can lose everything you own, apart from your clothes and the tools of your trade. If your business is run by a limited company, that company has a separate legal entity of its own, and if that entity goes bankrupt, the property of its owners cannot be seized to pay off its debts. You may lose everything that the company owns, but you do not lose your house, your car, your personal horses, or the contents of your personal bank account. It is for this reason that many small businesses are content to put up with the expense and inconvenience of running a limited company. (Incidentally, you may find bank managers are cagey about lending large sums of money to limited companies which have just been started, and they will probably require your personal guarantee on the loan.)

A final thought on bankruptcy. A creditor can start bankruptcy proceedings against you if you owe a comparatively small amount and fail to pay. What is not generally known is that at least half of the bankruptcy proceedings in the UK are brought by either the Inland Revenue against defaulting taxpayers, or by the DSS against people who do not pay insurance stamps. This latter is very easy for the small business owner to forget, but they will always catch up with you in the end!

One aspect of running your business as a limited company which needs careful consideration is whether you personally want to be employed or self-employed. If you are a sole trader, you will be self-employed, and will get all the tax advantages that this entails. But you will get very little in the way of social security and unemployment benefits, and for this reason you may prefer to be employed, which is easier to organise where a company is involved. There are also some major advantages attached to your pension arrangements. This is a very complex area, and you must discuss it in depth with your accountant before taking a decision. See Chapter 6 for more details.

Partnerships

I have already mentioned partnerships a couple of times, and I now ought to warn you that they are not a good idea, especially for those who are new to running a business. The main problem with partnerships is the concept known as joint and several liability. This means that each individual partner is personally liable for the debts of the partnership – all of them, not just their own share. You may have what you think is an equal partner, but that does not mean that your contribution is restricted to 50 per cent of any debts. If the other partner or partners cannot pay their share, the creditors will come to you. You can even be liable for a partner's personal debts if the creditors can put up a good case for those debts having been incurred for business purposes!

The second disadvantage is human nature. The business world is full of horror stories about partnerships that have gone wrong. The commonest relate to situations where one partner draws half the profits but does hardly any work; or uses the partnership's money for personal trading ventures, such as buying and selling horses. This wouldn't be too bad if the profits of those ventures went back into the partnership, but they usually do not!

You can do a certain amount to protect yourself from these disadvantages by getting your solicitor to draw up a formal partnership agreement which states who does what, who gets what, and who signs the cheques – and also that any other business activities of the partners do not constite part of the partnership.

Losses

Finally in this chapter, some thoughts on losses. From an accountant's point of view, a loss is not always the disaster it may appear to the lay person. If it goes on too long, the taxman will begin to wonder how you manage to eat regularly, and start to probe deeper, but on a short-term basis (like about four years) it may even turn out to be advantageous. The Inland Revenue get a bit tired of clever business people using 'hobby farms' as tax losses, but provided that you can prove you are running your business 'with a view to profit' they will not object too much. However, beware of those words, and if you get a letter from the Inland Revenue using them, be sure to consult your accountant before answering. Come to think of it, it is a good idea to consult him every time before talking or writing to them. They have a sneaky habit of asking superficially innocent but actually carefully worded questions that need equally carefully worded answers. If your registered business address is at your accountant's, and you keep your books there, you should avoid this sort of problem – and maybe even those awful visitations from the VAT inspector we've all heard about.

How can a loss be turned to advantage? Losses from one year can, in some circumstances, be set against profits from the next, and this reduces the tax on the profitable year. Remember that as a self-employed person you are still entitled to that personal allowance, which means you pay no tax on the first chunk of your income. If that allowance is £2,000, and your business shows a profit of £2,060 for the year after last year's loss has been deducted, you will only have to pay tax on £60.

Better yet, losses from one business can often be set against earned income from another source, with the same result. So, if you have a job and are running a business on the side, and it makes a loss, that loss can be used to reduce the tax liability from the job. A similar arrangement pertains if a married couple are taxed jointly, and one works while the other runs a business which makes a loss. And since the tax on the job will already have been paid by PAYE, the end result is a tax rebate.

Self-employed persons can also set losses from their first four years' trading against the income from the preceding three year's employment. And when it is all settled, you get one of the rarest things known to modern man – a cheque from the Inland Revenue.

5

Legal Matters

In any business, there are certain legal obligations which must be met, and running a stables is no exception.

Income Tax and National Insurance

The first obligation is that you must pay tax on any profits the business makes. The complex issues of what constitutes a profit, and how to minimise the tax due on it, have been covered in Chapter 4, so it will suffice to say now that this tax must be paid.

The next obligation is that anyone who works, and whose remuneration is above a certain level, must pay National Insurance contributions. This applies to the proprietor of the business as well as the employees. In the case of employees, the business must deduct these contributions from their wages and, after adding a contribution from the employer, must remit these sums regularly to the DSS, via the Income Tax offices. Income Tax must also be deducted from the wages, and these two amounts are added together and paid each month, in one cheque, to the Inland Revenue.

If there are no employees, or none whose remunerations reach the limits (which change each year with the budget) the proprietor may make other arrangements for paying these contributions. Where National Insurance stamps are concerned, the usual way to do this is to make a standing order through your bank to pay the necessary amounts at regular intervals. Alternatively, you can buy an actual DSS stamp each week from the Post Office and stick it onto a card provided by the local DSS office.

Income Tax on self-employed persons is usually assessed on an annual basis and then two six-monthly payments are made. The Inland Revenue used to do the assessment after it had seen your accounts, and will still do this if you ask, but it now prefers you to make a 'self-assessment'. You don't have to worry about this, as your accountant will do it for you. If you are slow in producing accounts and a tax return, the Inland Revenue may make an 'estimated assessment' and demand that you pay the tax on that. You can appeal against this, but any such appeal must soon be backed up by proper accounts. Incidentally, if you are slow in paying tax when it has been demanded, the Inland Revenue will charge you interest on the outstanding sum.

VAT

Next, there is the matter of Value Added Tax. VAT is one of those items that strike fear and trembling into the hearts of the inexperienced, but like most of these frighteners, it is comparatively simple to operate and, in the case of a stable, it is not likely to be too time-consuming, especially if you have done the preliminary work by filling in your cash books as suggested in Chapter 3. The possible complication lies in the initial registration, and deciding which part of your income is liable for VAT. Your accountant will help you with both of these problems.

As a general rule, any business which has a turnover above a certain level *must* register for VAT. (Note that 'turnover' means total takings, not profit.) Other businesses may register voluntarily, but this is usually only worthwhile for businesses that have a lot of purchases on which VAT has been charged, or those in the export business, for whom it is worth claiming back all the VAT which has been paid out. Since most of your expenses will be the sort which do not bear VAT (see below), you will probably not wish to register before you have to.

Businesses which are registered must collect VAT from their customers and hand it on to the Commissioners for Customs and Excise. On registration, each business is given its own VAT number, has to give its customers invoices which comply with the regulations, and then has to submit a quarterly return, with a cheque for the appropriate amount of VAT. (VAT paid out is deducted from that collected, and the net sum is what you have to pay.)

Animal feedstuffs bear no VAT, so it is only items such as the vet's bills, telephone bills and petrol which will allow you to claim anything back. However, all of the services you are providing your customers are liable to VAT. This may mean, if your turnover is above the limit and there is a smaller, unregistered yard down the road, that your customers will have to pay more than those of the other place. You may therefore consider it worthwhile lying to the VAT inspector about your turnover, but don't forget that Customs and Excise have powers to search your business premises and home if they suspect that you are on the fiddle. If and when they can prove it, you are guilty of fraud – which is a criminal offence. You will have to pay a big fine, or may even have to go to prison.

There is a way round the VAT business, which my local VAT office agrees is perfectly legitimate. However, if you are tempted to try it, first make sure that your VAT office agrees with mine. It goes like this.

As mentioned, animal feedstuffs are not subject to VAT. Actually they are zero rated, not exempt, but in this case the effect is the same. This means that a business which deals solely in these items need not register for VAT, even if its turnover is above the limit. Now, suppose you run two separate businesses (or even three, if you teach as well as keep liveries) one of which cares for the horses, and the other of which sell feedstuffs to the livery owners: there is a fair chance that the horse-care business will have a turnover well below the limit, which means that it can apply to the VAT office to de-register. Gone is all the hassle of filling in those returns, gone is giving the Customs and Excise all that money, and here is the real benefit – *without putting up your prices, you've just increased your profit margin by the amount of the VAT.*

Snags? Well, of course, there always are, but they are fairly minor. First I should stress that you *must* run two separate businesses. Trading as a sole trader under two different names will not do – the VAT inspector will say you are one business. But running one business as a sole trader and the other as a limited company is acceptable. Two limited companies would be even better. It means keeping two sets of books, but even that won't eat up all the extra profit. It also means training your livery clients to accept and pay two separate bills each month, but they will soon get used to that, especially if you point out to them that it is an alternative to putting up the price!

Relevant Acts

One other advantage to be gained by running several small businesses instead of one big one is that your employees can be spread between these businesses, and this may bring you exemptions under the *Employment Protection* and *Sex Discrimination Acts*. These issues are discussed further in Chapter 7.

I have mentioned elsewhere that you must comply with various pieces of legislation concerning your employees, customers, the public and the care of your horses. Other legislation of which you should be aware includes *The Animals Act, The Occupiers Liability Act, The Trades Description Act, The Sale of Goods Act* and the *Sale of Goods (Implied Terms) Act*. Since this is not a book on law, I will do no more than mention them, but you would be wise to check up on them and see where you stand.

Contract Law and Negligence

Two other areas you should check on, which I will mention briefly, are those of contract and negligence.

A contract is not necessarily a signed piece of paper – it is a certain type of agreement. A contract needs three conditions:

1) An offer: 'I will teach you to ride if you give me £15 an hour.'
2) Acceptance: 'I agree – I will pay you that.'
3) Consideration: The £15 per hour and the tuition.

Or: 'I will train you to pass BHS exams if you will work for me for no wages but your keep for one year.'

'I accept – I will do that.'

In this example the consideration is the work done, and the keep and training given.

'Can I have a ride on your horse?' 'Sure, go ahead' does not constitute a contract, for there has been no consideration.

A breach of contract arises when one of the parties involved does not do what was agreed, for example pay, or provide proper tuition. The aggrieved party can then sue, and if successful will either be awarded financial damages, or 'specific performance', which means that the other party must do what was agreed or be in contempt of court. This, at any rate, is the legal situation. In practical terms, suing is so expensive that the average person puts such unfortunate situations down to experience. However, there is always a chance that some interested body may decide to support a test case, so tread warily. It also works the other way – you might find yourself involved in a test case with backing from the Association of British Riding Schools (ABRS) or the British Horse Society (BHS).

Negligence is a potentially nastier area, but can be insured against. The issue of 'duty of care' of a proprietor is discussed in Chapter 6. Ask the ABRS for their leaflet on negligence and keep a wary eye out for dangerous situations and items on your premises. Don't ask pupils to over-reach themselves, or let them do so unsupervised.

If an accident does occur, enter all the details immediately in your accident book, including the names of everyone involved in or witnessing the incident, and the action you took. Admit nothing – be careful even of saying you are sorry, for this could be construed as an admission of guilt, as every motorist knows. If a claim is made, do no more than acknowledge it and state that it is being passed on to your insurers. Warn the insurers as soon as possible of situations from which a claim may arise. In the event of a death or 'major' injury (one which puts the victim in hospital for 24 hours) you must also report it to the Environmental Health Department. If you are unfortunate enough to have a death on your premises, you must report it immediately to the police.

Rates and Planning Permission

Finally, to areas where I can give no more than general guidelines, those of rates and planning permission. You must pay the rates demanded by your local council, but you can appeal for a re-assessment if you think they are too high. There are certain paths you can follow in an attempt to reduce them, but how effective these will be depends entirely on the local authority concerned. The best way is to go for an agricultural assessment, either by declaring you are a smallholding if you have enough land (usually 30 acres), or by keeping some cattle. Beef cattle may bring you some subsidies, or you may keep a registered dairy herd, which may not need to be more than two cows!

Think carefully before surfacing your car park, which might make it an amenity and raise the rates. And be careful with your manège, whether indoors or out. Some local authorities ignore outdoor schooling areas; others consider them business amenities and charge accordingly. An indoor manège may be considered an entertainment area if you use it too often for shows, but in some areas it can be assessed as an agricultural building. This is more likely if you keep cows, or it may require walls which do not reach the roof, or a hay store at one end.

Planning permission is needed for practically everything,

and it also affects the rates. If you want to erect a permanent building (just what constitutes a permanent building can also be open to interpretation), install a caravan, surface your car park or even change your roofing material, you must get planning permission. If you want to use 'premises', which term includes fields, for a different use than that currently listed, you must get 'change of use' permission, and this is not always easy. Some local authorities have extremely negative attitudes towards keeping horses.

Where both rates and planning permission are concerned, it is very much a case of finding out from other stable owners or independent surveyors what the local council's attitude is, *before you approach the authorities*. Once they've said no, it is very difficult to get them to change their minds, even if you amend your plans.

6
Insurances – Obligatory and Sensible

Obligatory Insurance

Everyone knows that all vehicles must carry third party insurance, but it is not so generally known that businesses must also carry certain insurances to protect their staff and the public.

EMPLOYERS LIABILITY

Employers liability insurance covers such items as unsafe working conditions or equipment, accidents to staff while they are working, or injury caused to them by your negligence. Not only are you obliged to carry this insurance, you must also prove you have it by displaying a certificate in a prominent place. Failure to do so could mean the authorities closing down your establishment.

PUBLIC LIABILITY AND THE DUTY OF CARE

If you are running an establishment open to the public, you must also carry public liability cover, to protect the public while they are on your premises. Many local authorities have a laid-down minimum amount of cover which you must have before they will grant you a riding establishments licence. The policy for this cover will almost certainly contain a clause to the effect that it is only valid where pupils are concerned if they are wearing a correctly fitted hard hat and proper shoes whilst riding. Most schools keep a stock of hats for pupils to borrow, but these do have a habit of disappearing, and you should make it clear that regular clients are expected to provide their own. You might like to display a notice stating that properly fitted hats must be worn, and disclaiming responsibility if they are not. But this notice must be where pupils can see it before they ride – otherwise the courts will not support your claim that the warning was given. The point of law in operation here is this: horse riding is known to be a risky occupation, and people who indulge in it are considered to be aware of and accepting that risk. However, you are a professional, and you also know of that risk, so you are expected to minimise it by insisting that all reasonable precautions are taken. This is called your 'duty of care'. Displaying that notice is evidence of your intention to minimise the risk, but if an injured pupil were able to say that she was not warned, you could be considered to be neglecting your duty of care.

Sensible Precautions

Now we have covered all the legal obligations on insurance, we can turn our attention to sensible precautions, by which I mean more insurance. Schools of business management will tell you that there is an alternative, which they call self-insurance. What this means is being exceedingly careful, and keeping a contingency fund to cope with disasters. Being a firm believer in Sod's Law, I prefer to wrap the protection of an insurance company around me. Sod's Law? It's the one that says dropped toast always lands butter side down, and it also decrees that any item which is not insured always gets lost, stolen or broken.

COMPREHENSIVE VEHICLE COVER

I have mentioned above that you must have third party insurance on your vehicles, but you may feel it more sensible to have fully comprehensive cover on them. In addition to the advantages of not having to pay for stolen or damaged vehicles this means that, in the event of problems, your insurance company gives you the money then sets about getting it from the third party, thus reducing the amount of hassle you suffer.

HIRING HORSEBOXES

Where horseboxes are concerned, you must be careful about whose horses you carry and on what terms. Many establishments transport their livery horses, not actually charging for it directly, but putting it on the livery bill. This is a very 'grey' area, so be careful about it. If you are carrying horses for 'hire and reward' without complying with all the necessary regulations relating to that trade, you can be in trouble with the Ministry of Transport – and with your insurance company, too.

FLOOD, FIRE AND STORM PROTECTION

If you keep large quantities of hay and straw about your premises, you may want to insure it against flood or fire damage. Since the insurance company knows the stock will be diminishing as the year progresses, this type of insurance is very cheap (about £1 premium for every £100 of hay), but beware of clauses on spontaneous combustion.

Insuring your premises against damage will cost about £2.50 per £1,000 of cover if they are brick, more if they are wooden. Insurance to cover storm damage will be about £10 per £1000, since wooden buildings and barns are especially vulnerable to high winds. Wooden buildings are also vulnerable to fire, and since stables tend to contain other hazards such as straw, fire insurance may be difficult to get without complying with strict conditions laid down by the insurance company. Sensible people have lots of fire extinguishers, and regular fire drills so everybody knows what to do – and an absolutely inflexible 'no smoking' rule.

If you are running a riding school, you will be able to get a block policy, covering all risks including mortality of horses, and third party.

LIVERY YARD OWNER'S INSURANCE

A special Livery Yard Owner's policy will protect you for your liability to the horses in your care, against such hazards as an icy yard which could cause an animal to slip and injure himself. It also covers you against your liability as the 'keeper' of the horse. Under *The Animals Act*, the person who is 'keeping' a horse, even though that person may not be the owner, is liable for any damage the horse does whilst in their care.

As to the insurance of the horses themselves, livery owners must insure their own. However, you can get a discount if you are insuring five or more of your own horses with one company. You will also find that most of the big insurance brokers will be happy to make you an 'introducer' so that you can earn commission by steering your clients in their direction. (This does not mean you have to be involved in making any necessary claims – the broker will handle those.)

Livery owners also usually insure their own tack. Tack is considered a 'target' risk by the insurance companies, and the premiums on it are quite high. If you want to insure large quantities, the insurance company might even send a representative along to check your security. Perhaps you could arrange for your dog to emerge from the tack room and bite him, just to convince him that you have a highly efficient guard dog!

PERSONAL INSURANCE

Having considered all the things that are likely to happen to your premises, equipment and animals, let us now consider yourself. If you are ill for any length of time it is likely that your business will suffer permanently, especially if you have no money coming in while you are unable to work. You may be able to get someone to take over running your business while you are ill, but will it make enough to pay both them and you? For this reason you may want to take out a Permanent Health Policy. Unlike a Personal Accident Policy, which only pays out for a limited length of time (at most two years) this takes you up to the age of 65. Such policies are not easy to get, because insurance companies are wary of them for the very reason you want them. They cannot cancel the contract to insure you until retiring age, no matter how often you may claim. The premium should be about 2 per cent – in other words, the annual premium will be the same as the potential weekly benefit.

You may also feel it wise to join one of the private medical insurance schemes, such as BUPA or PPP. These ensure that you receive prompt treatment at a time convenient to yourself, should you require an operation. Imagine trying to run your stables whilst feeling increasingly ill for the many months it can take to get treatment on the NHS. You may survive, but will your business?

I mentioned in Chapter 1 that you will be required to insure your own life if you have a large loan. There are a number of ways you can do this. The cheapest is called 'term' which pays out if you die within the fixed term of the policy, say five years. There is a version of this called '226a term', which still has tax relief on it, but it must run for a minimum of ten years and, ideally, until you retire. Neither of these policies is of any value to you while you are alive. Slightly more expensive is 'whole of life' which covers you until you die, at whatever age. This, unlike term, has a surrender value. The most expensive form is 'endowment' which is for a fixed term, at the end of which it pays out a lump sum. It also has a surrender value.

PERSONAL PENSIONS

If you are operating on a self-employed basis, you will be able to take out a personal pension plan. The tax advantages of these plans are enormous, for you effectively give yourself a substantial chunk of what you would otherwise have given to the taxman. You can put a high percentage of what the insurance companies call 'net relevant earnings' (the gross profit of your business after deduction of expenses but before tax) into your pension plan each year. But you are not committed to such a large premium every year if you do not have the money available; you can buy lump sum (called 'single premium') policies at any time, using up your tax allowances for the previous seven years.

If you are operating as a limited company and are taxed on a PAYE basis, your pension will be not a 'personal' but an 'executive' plan. In this case you can contribute considerably more than above, to such an extent that you can virtually eliminate any tax liability perfectly legally. As you might imagine, with such advantages, these schemes are extremely complex and you will need to consult both your accountant and a financial expert who is experienced with this type of insurance plan.

With both types of pension, you have the options of taking a pension at retirement, or leaving it to grow a little longer. And you don't have to make the decision on this until retirement. Both types have death benefits and a facility for a widow(er)s pension after you die.

There is another advantage of paying into a pension plan; you can use it to raise a loan. The security is the lump sum at retirement, and you can borrow up to fifteen times the annual contribution. These loans can be cheaper than other types, but once again you will have to consult an expert.

Where pensions and life insurance are concerned, you can get advice from two types of source. The first is from an organisation such as a bank or building society, which sells only its own financial products (and can thus advise only upon these. The other is an independent financial adviser (known as an IFA), who is able to sell and advise on products from the whole of the financial industry. Both are now rigidly controlled under *The Financial Services Act.* *

One final word on general insurances. Shop around a little before you buy. Ask friends which company of brokers they have found most reliable – for remember, brokers exist on the commission they get from the insurance companies, and this may influence their advice to you!

---

* The comments in this book on investments and investment-linked products are intended for information only, and are not meant to constitute investment advice.

7

Staff, Working Pupils and Hangers-on

No establishment of any size can survive without staff, for there is a limit to the number of horses any one person can care for. Although the person who runs a stable usually does her share of stable work and teaching, she cannot do her primary job – that of running things – unless she has the time and energy to devote to that function. Much stable work can be done by unskilled labour, and this is cheap and easy to obtain. Paying your accountant to do the paperwork that you were too tired to do, or paying a lawyer to get the authorities off your back when you have neglected your other obligations, is not cheap.

The cheapest labour of all comes in the form of working pupils, but even this is not totally free. Although they do not receive a wage, they must be fed and housed, and have time expended on them to teach them the skills for which they are exchanging their labour. You do not, however, have to make National Insurance contributions for them so long as they receive no financial remuneration above the fixed limit.

Employment Legislation and Contracts

As an employer, you have to comply with some statutory rules. The first of these involves the legislation that comes under the heading of Employment Protection. Like all such legislation, this tends to change fairly regularly, and you should check with your solicitor or accountant, who will be able to tell you which rules apply to your specific situation. As a rough guide, it says that you must give a contract of employment to each member of staff, and that you have to be careful about sacking anyone after they have been with you for twenty-six weeks. It also covers sick pay and leave.

The ABRS can help you by supplying some standard Contract of Employment forms, but the basics are as follows. You must list conditions of employment, hours to be worked, holiday entitlement, salary and periods of notice for ceasing the employment. The usual method of dealing with this is to give the employee two copies of this contract, requiring her to sign one copy as agreed and return it to you for your files.

While it is not a legal requirement, it would be a sensible precaution to make the same sort of arrangement with working pupils, for then neither they nor their parents can say that they did not understand what was expected of them. Nor, if you have a signed copy of this agreement in your files, can they sue you for breach of contract over such misunderstandings, always provided that you have kept your side of the bargain.

Employees who consider that they have been unfairly dismissed can take you to an Industrial Tribunal, where you may be ordered to reinstate them, or to pay them compensation. If the employee has been with you for less than twenty-six weeks; is a part-timer working less than a specific number of hours per week; is a close relative of yours; or is over retiring age, these provisions do not apply; nor do they apply if you have no more than three employees.

Employment legislation also covers the employee's right to belong to a trade union or professional association; and to maternity leave, pay whilst on such leave, and the right to return to her job after confinement.

The Equal Pay Act says that employees doing similar work must be paid equally, regardless of sex. *The Race Relations Act* says you may not discriminate because of race or colour, and *The Sex Discrimination Act* says that you may not discriminate between male and female employees when recruiting, training or promoting employees unless there is a 'genuine occupational qualification', or you have no more than four employees. The genuine occupational qualifications which would apply to stables are those of decency (usually related to sanitary facilities) or where staff live in and you cannot provide separate accommodation.

The Health and Safety at Work Act says that employers have a duty to provide and maintain safe machinery and systems of work for their staff (for example, chaff cutters); to provide safe handling, storage and use of any substance (for example, wormers and fertilisers); to provide safety information, training and supervision (in tasks such as stallion handling); to take proper care of the working environment and to provide adequate and safe access to and egress from working areas. All these provisions also apply to non-employed visitors (such as delivery drivers) and there are Health and Safety at Work Inspectors who have the power to enter your premises and ensure that you are complying with the Act. While most of these provisions were laid down to protect factory workers, you will see from the examples given that they can apply to stables as well.

Wages and Duties

If you have staff who are actually employed by you, rather than self-employed freelances, you must operate the PAYE scheme when calculating their wages. The local Inland Revenue office will provide you with all the necessary documentation, and show you how to operate it. Basically, it consists of deduction tables for tax and social security contributions, and a record card for each employee. Dealing with this is another of those tasks that is frightening in the idea of its complexity, but simple when you actually do it. You can get computer software or kits from stationers to help or, as I mentioned before, your accountant will do it for you. However you handle this side of things, wages should be paid on a regular basis – the same day each week or month – or staff are liable to become discontented.

Quite often, a member of staff will want to keep her horse in your yard, and you should think carefully before deciding how much to charge for this. Remember that the animal will be occupying space which could be used by a paying livery, and could also take up a disproportionate amount of the owner's time. It would be wise to include the agreement on this arrangement in her contract of employment.

No matter whether or not your staff are paid, or what hours of work are involved, it is essential that all parties concerned are clear as to what is expected of them, and these expectations should be adhered to on both sides. It is dishonest for an employer to expect an employee to work longer hours without some recompense.

Another area which should be carefully defined is that of the precise duties of each person. Ideally, each groom should have responsibility for specific horses. That way, not only do the horses have the mental security of knowing their groom (and getting some affection from her) but it is much easier for you to pinpoint any dereliction of duty. By the same token, the same stand-in should always be used when the regular groom is not available.

Looking at the matter from the other side, training schedules for working pupils should be laid down and adhered to. They work for training, not pay, and if they do not get it, they have a legitimate grievance. They could even sue you for breach of contract.

Staffing Structure and Deployment

The most important member of your staff is the one whom military people call 2 IC, which means second in command. It is essential to have someone you can trust to run things in your absence. Without her, you can never have a holiday, catch 'flu, go to a show or even down to the shops for a couple of hours. This person must not only be one you can trust, but someone whom the rest of the staff will respect and obey – for otherwise you could still return to chaos.

As to the sort of staff you will need, that depends on what you are doing. Grooms and teachers are fairly obvious, but had you thought of part-timers to feed the staff (who should muck out their own rooms), and to do the various bits of building maintenance that are always needed? Old-age pensioners are often happy to do this sort of work. Certainly, you can do such things yourself, but if you're paying a freelance teacher £10 an hour when a retired electrician costs £5 per hour, and you're fixing fuses when you could be teaching, you're wasting £5.

You will need some sort of contingency plan to cope with illness, whether your own or your staff's. As mentioned in Chapter 6, you would be wise to take out a policy to protect yourself from prolonged incapacity through illness or accident. Accidents are a constant hazard around horses, and since you are in charge and are likely to be the most experienced person available, it is you who will have to cope with any recalcitrant horse and take the subsequent risk of injury. If you are self-employed, you won't get much sickness benefit from the State, and even if you are employed and do get it, it isn't much to live on or pay your stand-in while you are incapacitated.

Sod's Law says that if anyone is going to get 'flu, gastro-enteritis or whatever bug is going round, everyone will get it, either all at once, or in quick succession. So you should have a list of 'call-onable' people up your sleeve in case the Fates decide they don't like you. There are also other precautions you can take. Insistence on simple, basic hygiene is one of them. It is all too easy for staff in a hurry to rush in and eat a sandwich for lunch without washing – when they have spent the morning mucking out. 'Yuck', you may say, but I've seen it done. There isn't a lot you can do about circulating tummy bugs, but you might like to consider 'flu jabs in the autumn, or keeping people with heavy colds away from others.

You should certainly keep a comprehensive first aid kit where everyone can get at it, and check it regularly to replenish items which have been used. The more people there are on your premises, the more staff trained in first aid there should be.

Rules and Regime

Far too many establishments allow their staff to work and meet clients in appallingly scruffy dress. This is not only off-putting to the clients, it is quite unnecessary. One appreciates that young grooms cannot afford a lot of clothes, but that is no excuse for their not being neatly turned out, with tidy hair. It should not prove too expensive for you to give them identical pullovers to wear in the yard, and it will do wonders for the general appearance of the place. If you do this, the pullovers will be tax-deductible and, if you are registered, you can also claim back the VAT on them.

I previously mentioned food and lodging for staff. While they will not expect accommodation to be palatial, it must be of a civilised standard. You cannot expect staff to give of their best if they are tired from a cold or uncomfortable bed, nor if they are not eating properly. Since working pupils are likely to be young, this latter really means you should ensure that they are getting a balanced diet. Left to their own devices they may try to exist on crisps and pop, or go to the other extreme and starve themselves for the sake of their figure.

Alcohol should be strictly restricted, if not completely banned. Drunks are notorious for starting fires, and it doesn't take much to get a teenager drunk. Furthermore, hangovers are not conducive to good horse-care.

Sex is a definite No-No. Not only does it frighten the horses (or so Oscar Wilde tells us), but it plays hell with discipline. Between staff, it, or its preliminaries, waste working time; between staff and clients it is even worse, and between either and proprietor. . .!

Where working pupils are concerned, just remember that you stand *in loco parentis*. You may not want to be bothered with what the girls are doing at night, but do you really fancy explaining to Mummy and Daddy how little Susan comes to be pregnant?

Unpaid Helpers

It often happens, especially at riding schools, that unpaid helpers accumulate – or rather helpers who wish to be paid in rides rather than money. In most cases, these will be horse-mad young girls. Your first concern should be to establish that there is no parental objection to their prolonged presence on your premises. The next should be, as in the case of working pupils, that specific rights and duties are laid down, for example two days work for one hour's ride. But be careful on this point: payment in kind is still payment, and there is legislation on employing children.

Whilst two or three such girls can be really useful, greater numbers tend to mess about together instead of working. They annoy clients with their giggling, and get under the feet of those who are trying to work. If the giggling grows to shrieking and rushing about, as it often can, then the horses will be upset and other harm can be done. Messing about in the hay shed spoils hay; grooming kit gets lost, tools can get left about and you could end up with a horse puncturing a sole on an abandoned rake, or worse. What it boils down to is remembering that you are in charge, and putting a stop to these high jinks before they get started.

The Staff-Boss Relationship

Being the boss is often thought of as a cushy number. All you have to do is tell other people what to do, and rake in the money. But those who see it that way forget the other side of the picture. You cannot tell someone what to do unless you know how to do it yourself, for how will you know it has been done correctly? The person who is doing the work has only four or five horses to deal with – you must oversee perhaps twelve or twenty, and the ultimate responsibility for their welfare rests with you. You are the one who must ensure that the owners and pupils are kept content, or there will be no money to be raked in. And since yours is the name on the loan document that provided the capital to make the whole thing possible, so you are the person who must shovel back out the money you have just raked in.

Disgruntled staff can do more harm than you could believe. One hopes you will never encounter anyone warped enough to injure a horse deliberately, but even without that intention, animals can be upset mentally by a bad atmosphere or brusque handling. Sullen staff are also off-putting to clients, so it's up to you to sort out their problems fast, or to get rid of them equally fast.

If you find that your staff are under the impression that they are earning your living for you, you've been going about things the wrong way. The old: 'I'm in charge. Don't ask questions, just get on with it' routine is as outmoded as the crinoline. Today's approach is the more effective one of teamwork, with the boss as the leader of the team. Just remember that wages for those who work with horses are very low compared to what they can get elsewhere. They work with horses because they like doing so, not because of the financial rewards, and if they don't get job satisfaction, they will soon begin to wonder why they are not working nine to five in a cosy office. It's up to you to make sure they do get job satisfaction and stay as part of your team, or you may wake up one morning and find you've got to do twenty horses all on your own.

8

Riding Schools and Teaching

The basic requirements for running a riding school are infinite patience and a taste for dealing with the public, since you cannot pick your customers as you might with a livery yard. Since you can hire teachers, being able to teach yourself is not essential. It is, however, useful, especially if all your staff go down with 'flu on a Friday evening when you are fully booked for the weekend.

Setting Tuition Levels

You must first decide the level of tuition you want to offer, and assess whether you can get enough pupils at that level to make the venture pay. What most prospective teachers just do not realise is that about 90 per cent of riding school clients have, to put it mildly, limited ambition as far as horses are concerned. They want a little exercise, a chance to see the countryside the lazy way, or something to boast about in the office. They are not aware of, nor interested in, the finer points of equitation, and will soon abandon a school whose instructors insist on a perfect position at the walk in favour of one where they can pop over some jumps or gallop through the woods as soon as they can stay on board. Since this type of person seems to be the one who can afford to pay regularly for lessons, there are obviously plenty of establishments to cater for them, and you may care to join their ranks with your school. If you are not of that persuasion, don't scorn those who are - we're talking about making a living, remember, not reforming the world.

Such yards do have their own problems, not least those of slipping standards. It is easy, when nobody appreciates that you do things well, to decide not to bother, and the slope from there to getting complaints from the RSPCA is steep and slippery. There is usually a high turnover of staff at these schools, too. Young teachers with high ideals become restless when faced with a succession of pupils whose mental attitude is matched only by their poor proprioceptive sense. And the horses soon learn that they can take advantage, and do so. This doesn't help the hapless instructor, who rarely has time, even if she has the inclination, to re-school them. The only answer is to sell the offender, and hope the replacement will not be so bad.

The higher the level of instruction offered, the fewer prospective pupils there will be in any given area. Those schools that offer instruction above, say, medium dressage standard, need such a large catchment area that they must adapt by offering instruction on a course rather than an hourly basis. In such circumstances the pupils will often want to bring their own horses, so accommodation for horses as well as riders must be available. It's a whole new can of worms at this level, and not one for beginners to open.

The more usual way of offering high-level tuition is to employ a good freelance instructor on a 'once a week' basis. These instructors soon acquire a following of enthusiastic pupils, who will turn up every week come hell, high water or blizzard, and they are useful if your working pupils want to take exams and you have no one on your full-time staff with adequate experience to prepare them.

There are establishments which get most of their bread and butter from paying students on three-, six- and twelve-month courses, but again this is a rather specialised area, for it is very much dependent upon reputation and the pass rates of previous pupils. It is also dependent on national and local politics, since many of these students will be paid for and supported by various youth training schemes. It only takes a policy decision from some bureaucrat to drastically reduce or even completely stop your flow of income from these students.

You might like to specialise in teaching children. Many schools, especially the more serious-minded, do not wish to be bothered with them until they are quite advanced or above a certain age, so there could be an opening for such specialisation in your area. Children do represent a perhaps steadier income than adults, for they will want to ride during school holidays as well as at weekends, and may even be able to come after school in term time. However, both you and your staff will have to be prepared to cope with children *en masse*. It needs extra patience and eyes in the back of your head if you are to keep both your establishment and your sanity intact. It needs a fairly tough skin too, for every revolting little brat has a mother who dotes on it. As anyone who has ever judged a leading-rein class knows, these ladies are dangerous! Most children and their parents are charming, of course, but there always seems to be one 'orrible one in every batch, and it requires a genuine love of children if you are to resist the temptation to bury this sort in the manure heap.

Horses and Facilities

For any form of riding school you will, of course, need some horses, and they are probably the worst headache of all. The type you need is no longer as cheap as in days gone by, and is getting rarer. I mean the kind, sensible plodder, who is easy to feed and stays sound. He is rare because of his high meat value, for this sort of horse is usually on the chunky side, and no oil painting. Today's fashion is more towards quality, which is super as a general state of affairs, but the quality horse is really not a good bet for a riding school. Delicacy of physique apart, his temperament is rarely suitable.

You'll need a couple of weight-carriers, but think very carefully before getting any really big horses. Unless you have a steady stream of very big men riding, the extra food a big heavyweight needs can easily outweigh his usefulness. Medium-sized cobs are much better buys, as they can be ridden by both lightweight and heavyweight pupils.

It is also worth remembering that very pale coloured horses, such as white greys or palominos, whilst very attractive to customers, often require much more grooming time than darker animals to keep them clean.

The degree of schooling your horses will need is directly related to the level of teaching you offer, but the frequency and amount of re-schooling needed is in inverse ratio to the standard of instruction. A teacher with high standards will not permit her pupils to allow their mounts to develop bad habits, and thus the degree of schooling will remain fairly constant. A poor instructor will either not care or not notice that a horse is developing bad habits until it is too late, and the horse has taken to attacking his fellows, cutting across the school or depositing his rider. This sort of vice, or the 'I know I can get away with it, this is a beginner' idleness is very difficult to cure, and the horse isn't exactly saleable either.

It is a good idea to keep a record of your school horses. Note how much work they do; how much feed and attention they need; how often they need the farrier or the vet; whether they cost a lot in tack or rug replacements; whether they are box-wreckers. Make a point of assessing these factors at regular intervals. What you are trying to establish for each horse is whether he is earning or costing you money. If it is the latter, you should harden your heart and 'out' him as soon as possible.

Record-keeping of this sort is easy enough. If you make daily entries in a large diary as they occur (Vet – Cascade, wormed, anti-tet/'flu boosters £56; Kipper – rasp teeth £18; Billy – torn rug), it is then a simple matter to transfer these details to each horse's record card once a month, or whenever you do your other office work. For a sample record card, see Appendix 4.

The ideal horse for any riding school, assuming that he is temperamentally suitable, is a part-livery. He costs you very little, if anything, to keep, and he isn't tying up your capital in horseflesh or accoutrements. He has only to work a few hours a week to earn the difference between part-livery and full livery, then anything else he earns after that is pure profit.

Unfortunately, you can't depend on these horses being around for too long. They usually belong to a novice rider, who has just progressed to the stage where she wants her own horse, but can't quite afford to pay full livery. The reason such horses don't stay available is that the owner eventually realises that she will not progress in her riding unless her horse progresses with her, and that means preventing him being ridden by all and sundry. At this point she either gives up and sells the horse, or puts him on full livery. Either way, you will lose the use.

You will need some decent tack for your horses. *The Riding Establishments Act* requires that it shall be safe and not injurious to the horse. Your good reputation requires that it should be clean, in good repair and fitted properly. Knots in throat-lashes or girths are not uncommon sights at some establishments, and even the complete novice is repelled by this sort of thing.

These days, it is virtually essential to have an indoor school, or at least a properly constructed outdoor one, with good lighting and good footing. Obviously, although more costly, the former is better, as it enables you to continue teaching in all weathers and also after dark. Weekday evening lessons are popular with working adults, who tend to come on a more regular basis than weekend riders. Horses have got to be fed regardless of the weather, and if a nasty day keeps the clients away, how can you afford to keep them as well as yourself?

Professional Associations

You may not feel that you need British Horse Society recognition, but this is no reason to be short with the local BHS representative. You may regard this person as a nosy busybody, especially if your place is not up to scratch, but what they are trying to do is improve the lot of the horse and the horse person generally. If you don't approve of that, shame on you! Anyway, who do you suppose makes most of the complaints to the council when it is licence renewal time?

What I would strongly advise you to do is join the Association of British Riding Schools. This organisation is run by professional stable owners, who know from experience the problems you are likely to encounter. They will help you with advice, standard forms of contract, many leaflets and with the power of their large membership. A good example of this was a situation in Scotland when the rating authorities suddenly reassessed all the riding schools, and issued them with bigger rating demands than before. Individual stable owners would have found this expensive, time-consuming and difficult to fight, but the BHS and ABRS were able to get these rates reviewed again and substantially reduced. Wouldn't you like that sort of backing? Incidentally, you don't actually have to run a riding school to be a member; they will accept livery stables as well, and your subscriptions will be tax-deductible.

The ABRS is also an excellent source of advice on complying with *The Riding Establishments Act*. Since there are books dealing specifically with horses and the law, I will not go into too much detail here, but basically the Act applies to any establishment which keeps horses for hire or teaching purposes, and says, amongst other things, that:

- You must have a Riding Establishment Licence. (This comes from the local council, after an inspection, and is renewable annually.)
- Horses must be in good health, and suitable for the purposes kept.
- Horses must be fed, stabled, bedded and shod adequately.
- Horses must be cared for properly, and veterinary first aid equipment must be kept available.
- Adequate storage must be provided for forage, bedding, stable equipment and saddlery.
- Persons supervising rides, lessons or the business itself, must be at least 16 years old.
- The licence holder must have proper insurance cover for both clients and the public.

You can be fined for offending against any of the above rules, and/or have your licence taken away. (The list above is not exhaustive, but merely intended to give you an idea of the provisions of the Act, and you should obtain a copy and make sure that you understand it.)

Arrangements for Lessons

You will need to give some thought to your timetables, especially with regard to the separation of riders of varying degrees of competence. Keeping in mind that the teacher who takes the advanced pupils may not want to take the beginners, there are a number of ways this can be done. You could start the day, or half-day, with beginners, working up to advanced riders as the day progresses. This could also apply to evenings, when you might have classes at 7, 8 and 9 p.m. Alternatively, you could reserve certain days or half-days for each category, have one day set aside for jumping lessons, or whatever. The latter plan does make the best and most economical use of specialised instructors, most of whom will prefer to do a half or whole day rather than a couple of hours here and there.

For your actual lesson bookings, you will need a fairly complex book, with provision for times, horses' and riders' names, and an indication of the payment. The easiest type to operate are the loose-leaf books as used by hairdressers, which have horizontal lines for times, and vertical columns for each horse. All you have to do is put a rider's name in the appropriate place, and you can see at a glance which horses are to be used for which lessons. You can draw a line in each box where you do not want a horse to be used, or strike out his whole column if he is off work that day.

One of the best organised places I know has this type of system, and also has a card which the client keeps. This card has thirteen lines, to state the time and date of the next lesson, and the instructor signs it when the client pays. Clients pay for twelve lessons and get the thirteenth free – if the card has been filled in properly. Other establishments require the client to pay before the lesson, and one that I know of even gives the client a token on payment, which has to be handed over to the instructor before they are allowed on a horse.

Almost all schools have a rule that lessons not cancelled by a certain time (24 hours notice, usually) must be paid for. This, however, is difficult to enforce, unless you have some sort of card system. The only other alternative I can think of is to sell regular clients a block of lesson tickets in advance, which will at least mean they will not miss a lesson for a trivial reason, like a last-minute reluctance to come out on a cold night.

You might also like to consider offering a video service to your more serious pupils. While you won't want to use video for every lesson, you could make this service available on a weekly or monthly basis, in which case you can hire a freelance instructor with their own video equipment, instead of having to buy and insure your own. Anyone who has used video as a teaching aid will know what a superb aid it is. Pupils can actually see what they are doing wrong, and this visual impact produces results immediately, instead of taking weeks as can be the case from a vocal description of the problem. (Even this presupposes an articulate instructor who is able to change her terminology to make sure *every* pupil understands the words she uses.) Video also teaches the instructor a great deal, especially with the use of slow motion applied to such problems as jumping falls and refusals.

One last thing you need to do when running a riding school is keep your eyes open all the time. Hopping horses, broken down buildings, tatty tack, grubby grooms and irritable instructors soon upset clients, and they go away, never to return with their purses again.

9

Liveries

Keeping other people's horses at livery is the easiest of all the horse businesses to enter, for it requires no licences and no qualifications – other than the ability to persuade prospective clients that you know what you are doing. I have chosen these words deliberately, for while to the educated rider the most desirable livery stable proprietor is one who is knowledgeable about horses, there are many stables which survive purely through the ignorance of their clients.

Targeting a Clientele

This is also a horse business which many people drift into in a small way, realising later that they can make a living out of it and then moving to larger premises. It may be, when you are looking for a place to keep your own horse, that you find a small yard of three or four boxes, and decide to offset your own expenses by sub-letting, and things just grow from there.

There are certainly plenty of horse owners who want to have their animals looked after, and are willing to pay for the service. The amount of service they require, and of course what they will be prepared to pay for it, will depend on their financial status.

At the top of the scale you will get those business people whose main interest is competing, who will be prepared to pay substantial amounts to have their horse looked after. Here, the total responsibility for the animal's welfare and fitness will lie with the stable. The animal must be fed, groomed and exercised properly and produced on competition days ready for the rider to climb on board. He must be turned out immaculately for competitions; if the owner does not have time herself, his schooling must be maintained; and in many cases the owner will also require a fair amount of hand-holding to calm pre-competition nerves. Such owners usually expect you to devote a high proportion of your personal time to them, so you will not be able to cater for many of them – which is one of the reasons you have to charge a lot. However, they do represent a source of additional income in the way of introductory commissions, since they tend to spend a lot on equipment, new horses, and tuition.

Ordinary full livery caters for the client who will want to ride more than once a week, but who is not able to look after her own horse. This horse must be fed, groomed and possibly exercised, his stable cleaned, his shoeing attended to and his tack cleaned. It is usual to include periodic veterinary nursing among these services at no extra charge.

The next level is called 'do it yourself' livery, usually costing substantially less than full livery. The horse is housed, fed, turned out and caught up again, and that is all. The owner rides, mucks out, grooms and cleans her own tack, and must arrange her own shoeing and veterinary attention – though I do know of one place that includes 'hygienic grooming' in its services. This interesting phrase means that if the horse injures himself whilst grazing, they will hose the mud off the wound when they discover it, but do no more unless paid extra. However, before you get too indignant about this, as was my first reaction, remember that this place is cheap because it does not have any staff to pay, which means no one is available to perform these extra services.

There are, of course, many establishments that offer some or all of these services for varying prices. Some have useful facilities to offer instead of horse care, so it is up to the owner to choose what she wants for her money, and the intended proprietor to decide what is the most profitable to provide.

It is generally thought that putting up fees to provide a

reasonable profit will immediately cause a total loss of clients. Unless the service you provide is so lousy that the only reason your clients stay with you is that you are dirt-cheap, this is just not true. Clients keep their horses at a specific place because they like the service, because you help them with their particular interest, because you have an indoor school, or because you are the easiest for them to reach, and they will think very carefully before losing these advantages for the sake of a couple of pounds.

Half- or part-livery is an arrangement offered by many riding schools. Here the fees will be between half and three-quarters of the full livery charge, and the horse is cared for as though he were on full livery. The balance of the fee is made up by using the horse in the school on lessons, usually for a set number of hours per week. It is especially important that areas of responsibility as well as hours of usage are clearly agreed by both parties. Some riding schools don't allow their part-livery owners to use their own horses at all at weekends – it never ceases to amaze me that they get away with it! No doubt these schools also insist that the owner pays all the vet's bills, regardless of who was in charge of the animal when he was injured, and then have the effrontery to charge full livery while the animal is off work. Add to this the fact that the owner provides and maintains the tack and pays the whole cost of shoeing . . . . this can all be summed up easily enough: play fair and don't push your luck!

Services and Agreements

In any livery arrangement, it is fundamental to the interests of both parties that there is a clear understanding of what is to be done for the price paid, how frequently this price is to be paid and who carries the responsibility for what. A wise stable proprietor will have a simple form of agreement drawn up, and get each owner to sign a copy of it as proof that they agree to the terms. Such a simple contract, though it may seem excessive to those not legally minded, will prove invaluable if you have trouble with non-payers. More on that shortly, but amateur horse owners are notoriously inclined to remove their animals while you are out, then refuse to pay the bill on the grounds that you were not looking after the animal properly. With this tendency in mind, many stable owners require their livery clients to pay each month in advance. For the same reason I strongly advise you to ensure that your clients pay their own vet's, farriery and tack repair bills, instead of you paying it and putting it on their bill. Even if they do not cause trouble over the payment, you are still having to lay out your own money on their behalf for no return, when it could be more usefully employed elsewhere.

Another problem frequently encountered is suspicion over whether or not a horse is getting all the feed that has been paid for, and this becomes especially complicated where vitamin supplements and other additives are concerned. Since each owner is likely to have her own ideas on which additive is best, this is not easily resolved, and you are likely to end up with a bucket or tin for each horse, and the consequent irritation of having to open each one at feeding time. However you deal with the actual issuing of these items you should, for the reasons mentioned above, insist that the owners buy these additives themselves.

I mentioned above the possibility of getting your livery clients to pay in advance. While this might engender a little bad feeling in the early days, it does avoid the problems of dealing with clients who do not pay. Such people fall into two categories – those who have removed their horses, and those who have not. With the latter you are in a slightly better position, for you can claim what is termed a lien on their horse or tack. This means that you do not release their property until they have paid their debt. In some cases (check with a solicitor) you may be entitled to sell their property to regain what is owing. You must, however, remit any balance to them. This course of action is fairly easy when the property involved is inanimate, but not so easy when it is a horse. You could padlock the stable door, to prevent the horse being taken for a ride and not coming back, but such action is likely to cause some very nasty feeling. At the very least, the offended debtor is going to bad-mouth you around the district. It is easier, perhaps, to claim and sell the tack.

If the horse has been removed, you are in the same position as any business with outstanding debts, and the same courses of action are open to you. These have been explained in Chapter 2, but in any such event you will need to establish properly that the debt is due – and this is why you should get that agreement on terms and conditions signed.

Some establishments, especially DIY yards, require their clients to supply their own stable furniture: buckets, haynets, saddle soap, etc., but all should expect them to provide their own grooming equipment, and to be scrupulous in its exclusive use on the animal for whom it is intended.

Another area in which you may have to be firm is use of facilities. If, for instance, you allow your clients to use your jumps, you might like to think of making a charge for that use. They are expensive to replace, easily broken (especially cavalletti) and somehow no one ever seems to know how it happened, let alone being prepared to pay for a replacement. You may like to consider adding something to the winter bills for use of school lights if clients have free use of the school. They'll all agree to put something in the box for every hour they use the school, and swear that they have done so, but somehow the contents of the box always fall short of the electricity bill. The only answer to this is to have a slot meter installed.

Long-term clients will feel they are entitled to a little extra consideration, and they are right. A high turnover of clients is usually a sign that there is something wrong with a yard, and the news soon gets around. On the other hand, it might just mean you are a bad chooser of clients, and collect a lot of bothersome ones who do not stay anywhere very long. You are entitled to refuse to keep any horse who requires extra work or special treatment or at least, to charge extra for those services. (We all know the client who insists that her horse must have his haynets soaked, or bed down on wood chips when all the others are on straw.) You should certainly make it clear that owners of horses who habitually wreck the joint will be expected to pay extra for that, too.

Another point which I have rarely encountered in practice, but would have thought was plain common sense, is the isolation of new horses when they first arrive. Who knows what a newcomer could be carrying in the way of disease? Your other clients will be justifiably annoyed if a newcomer infects their horses with 'flu, or contaminates the paddocks with worms.

In the interests of some privacy for yourself and the horses, it is wise to lay down open hours, and ensure that everyone sticks to them, or you will get no peace. Many yards have one 'closed' day per week, when the horses and most of the staff can have a well-earned rest. This is one of the areas where you may have to be firm with novice owners. They often tend, through ignorance rather than deliberate callousness, to abuse their animals, and often indirectly, others as well. Anyone who has seen a whole yard of horses flinch when a noisy child rushes about shouting while mother rides will know what I mean. If you haven't got the guts to ensure that the horses in your care are treated properly, then you shouldn't be in this business – and indeed, you probably won't be for long, for the horsy grapevine will soon spread the news.

10

Getting Organised – Yard and Office

Assuming that you know your subject, looking after horses is comparatively easy – when only two or three are involved. When numbers increase beyond this, it becomes less easy, and by the time you have more than a dozen horses in your care you can no longer rely on your memory to ensure that everything is done properly. This is the point at which you need to sit down and have a careful think about ways to organise everything to run as smoothly (and economically) as possible.

Saving Time and Money

I've already said that each member of staff should look after specific horses. While this is sensible enough, she will waste a lot of time and energy if her horses are spread all over the yard, and their tack and other kit is spread all over the tack room. I have always felt that a series of small sheds, one to each four horses, say, would be a good idea. Then each girl would have her own shed handy to her horses – and the chances of tack thieves stealing everything at one fell swoop would be much reduced.

There will be many other similar areas where time can be saved and irritations reduced. Thought should also be given to bulk buying in order to save money. Economists call this 'economies of scale', and these can be effected in other areas, besides the obvious one of feed. In a large yard you are bound to need regular replacements of items such as buckets and brooms, so you might just as well buy a dozen at a time. No need to go to a wholesaler - just point out to local shops that they have the option of selling you a dozen at a reduced price, or none at all.

Organise visits from a farrier on a regular basis, say every week or fortnight. If you have twenty horses, and he comes every week, there will always be four or five for him to do, and you will rarely have to call him out for emergencies. Treat him well - he knows you need him more than he needs you, and he is worth looking after. Give him a decent weatherproof place to work, with a proper floor and good lights, and keep him plied with hot and cold drinks according to the weather. And don't let your clients mess him about over payment.

The same consideration applies to vets, and they will also appreciate hot water and a clean towel. Try not to panic and call them out unnecessarily in the middle of the night, and follow their instructions on treatment to the letter. That way, when do you have a real emergency, they will know it is genuine and respond immediately.

While you may not care to dwell on subjects like the knacker-man, you are the one who may have to call him, and oversee his task. Nasty, I know, but if the casualty is a livery horse, the owner is going to be extremely upset, and looking to you for help. For heaven's sake don't upset the knackerman. You may not care for the way he makes his living, nor for the fact that many of the horses he slaughters are healthy, useful animals, but do you really fancy digging a hole big enough for a horse?

Organisation and Communication

Although your main task will be to oversee and delegate, there will be many jobs you still have to attend to, with the consequent problem of remembering them all. The answer to which is: don't try to - write it down! Every well-organised person I know keeps a list of things to do, putting each job down as they think of it, and crossing it off when it is done. Grade each job: A for 'urgent', B for 'today', C for 'this week', D for 'some-

time'; then you won't do the easy jobs first and have a last-minute panic because an urgent job has been overlooked.

Do make proper arrangements for receiving messages. Telephone answering machines are now quite cheap, depending on the degree of sophistication you want, but they usually mean you have to call people back, which costs more, unless your recorded message states that you will not do this, but can be reached at a certain time. In any case, it is certainly worth setting down 'office hours', when people know that they can reach you. Additional phones in strategic places avoid frantic dashes to answer the only one, but if you have one in your indoor school, it should be where it can be reached from horseback.

You may think that the obvious answer to communications is a mobile phone but, while useful, these do have disadvantages. Not least of these is that they tend to be expensive to use. They are also extremely desirable to thieves. There are several other points relating specifically to horses: the nervous animal who has hysterics when the phone in your pocket rings; the phone that rings just as your a pupil approaches a tricky jump; the phone that is constantly going wrong because of dust, and so on.

Feeding

One major area which requires thought is feeding. This involves what to feed, what quantities to buy and how to store it. I've already discussed the wisdom of buying hay off the field, and the same applies to straw. These items are comparatively easy to store, needing only to be stacked carefully and, if outside, covered with a rick sheet. Corn, which is also cheapest if bought in bulk at harvest time, needs to be kept at the right humidity, or else it will sprout or rot – and this is not so easy to arrange. If you do have the chance to buy in bulk from a farmer, he may agree to store it for you, but he will probably charge you. You've just got to do the arithmetic to be sure that bulk purchase is the cheapest way to do it. Bulk corn, even if it is only a two-week supply, is always cheaper because it has not been bagged – but you'll need a weighbridge ticket to check the weight received.

You may like to do your own corn-crushing and chaff-cutting to save expense, but consider the time it takes, the cost of machinery and the electricity before you decide it is cheaper. Another false economy I have encountered is that of feeding boiled whole barley. Certainly the barley is cheaper to buy than crushed oats, but what about the electricity needed to boil it?

Precautions should be taken to prevent wasting foodstuffs. Keeping hay at a distance and bringing each day's supply to the yard means that it all gets used, instead of being trodden into the floor. It also makes it easier to keep control of loose binder twine.

Hard feed should be kept locked up and stock checked regularly, for it is too easy for sacks to 'walk'. It also needs to be protected from moisture and rats, so bins will be required. Proper feed bins are costly, and dustbins are too small – the best makeshift I've seen is fifty-gallon oil drums, with a hinged wooden lid. A final thought – since some spillage is inevitable, so why not convert this waste into eggs with the help of some chickens?

It is amazing how many stable proprietors regard their fields as exercising or schooling areas, instead of feed production areas. I don't mean to suggest making your own hay, for that is a chancy business best left to farmers. What I'm talking about is grass, as a source of both protein and roughage. Every square metre of pasture that is growing weeds or the wrong type of grass is wasted; and every field that is not properly fertilised is partly wasted. All this waste means that you must spend more on hay and hard feed. Failing to pick up droppings, or harrowing to spread them, means spending more on wormers – and one could also question the desirability of constantly subjecting your animals to these drugs.

The final problem associated with feeding a lot of horses is disposing of the end product. Provided that your bedding is straw, this can be sold in bulk to mushroom growers, or in small quantities to individual local gardeners. (If you can find a local allotment society, it is possible to sell manure by the trailer-load.) If both ideas fail, a local farmer may like it, and he might swap it for straw. Wood chips are more difficult, as they are no use for fertiliser. The only answer is to burn them, which means having a safe place to do that, and enough storage space to allow for rainy periods.

Yard Layout and Saving Labour

You will be fortunate indeed if you are able to plan and build your own stables, but then you will be able to have them just as you want. Personally, I am a keen fan of the American barn system, with boxes down both sides of a large building. The doors open onto a wide aisle, and staff work completely under cover. Horses can be tied in the aisle for grooming or while their boxes are cleaned, and the whole thing is warmer in the winter and easier to illuminate efficiently. These barns are often attached to an indoor school, so there is no need to go out in bad weather, and they incorporate many labour-saving devices.

While the opportunity of building your own yard is rare, the wisdom of using all possible labour-saving devices is still valid. It is pointless for you or your staff to spend your valuable time on such mundane tasks as carrying buckets of water when there are other ways of watering horses. Automatic drinkers or individual taps recessed into the walls of the boxes, or a pistol grip on a long hose are all much quicker – and you don't spill water down your boots, either. Mangers near doors save a horse-dodging journey across a box and back, and polythene lift-out mangers are easier to clean than permanent fixtures. All that is needed is a little thought, and sometimes a little expenditure. But it is worth it, if your thinking and spending allows you to employ one less groom, or to spend more time doing the important jobs instead of the menial tasks.

Office and Equipment

Exactly what you will need in the way of an office, and office equipment, will obviously be dependent on the scale of your activities. If all you are doing is running a small livery yard, you won't need much more than a diary, a basic set of accounting books and somewhere to keep receipts for the items you have purchased. All of this can be kept in a big cardboard box and your kitchen table will serve as a desk for the times when you have to do some paperwork. However, if you are running a big riding school, with a couple of dozen school horses, some liveries, staff, working pupils, and a regular programme of shows, you are going to need something much more complex.

Most establishments fall somewhere between these two examples, but whatever the size of your business, the trick is to have enough equipment to get the administrative jobs done efficiently, but not so much that it is costing you more than it need do.

If at all possible, you should have a place which won't be used for anything else, set aside for office work. This way, there will always be somewhere to put papers so that they won't get lost and, unless you have undisciplined children, you will be able to leave things so that you can return to them and carry on from where you left off.

A big mistake that many people make when they start up in business is to spend a lot of money on expensive office equipment. A new desk, chair, filing cabinet and so on can easily set you back a four-figure sum, and such items won't do the job any better than second-hand versions. If money is particularly tight, you can create a very acceptable desk by resting a piece of kitchen work-top on a pair of two-drawer filing cabinets. Alternatively, you can buy office equipment extremely cheaply at auctions – although this is perhaps not the best place to buy machinery such as typewriters or computers unless you have the expertise to check them out first.

Whether or not you need a computer depends on the volume of repetitive tasks you do. Enthusiasts will tell you that a computer will do anything better than the 'old-fashioned' manual methods, but this is not true. They don't do it better – just faster, and then only if a lot of identical tasks are involved.

If you want to produce a set of 200 address labels four times a year for sending out show schedules, a computer will certainly do it much quicker than manual typing or handwriting the envelopes, once it has the names and addresses on a file. But if all you need is to produce six livery bills a month, by the time you've turned on the computer, started the right program, found the right file and turned on the printer, you could have handwritten the bills, addressed the envelopes and stuck the stamps on them.

The real problem with computers is that they are not as easy to use as the enthusiasts tell you. To read the advertisements and computer magazines, you'd think it is easy-peasy, but it isn't – or not when you are a complete beginner. It is very easy to press the wrong key, or accidentally press two keys together, and find something totally weird has happened. Even after ten years of using computers for word-processing, accounting, data collection, and doing various program adaptations, I can still find I've done something which results in spending the next half-day on the phone to a help-desk trying to sort it out.

Of course, if you are already computer-literate, or have a spouse or close friend who is, you won't have any problems, and you'll be aware of what the machines can do. But if you don't have that experience, you should expect to spend many tens of hours acquiring it – or else abandon the idea and stick to pen and paper.

Some of the tasks a computer can do for a stable are:

- Book-keeping and accounting work, including wages and VAT returns.
- Organising everybody's time with diary and organiser programs.
- Keeping databases of all your horses' health or competition details, and of all your clients' details. (If these include anything other than names and addresses, you'll have to

register under the *Data Protection Act.*)

• Producing address labels for sending out show schedules, information about advanced tuition clinics, etc.

• Printing invoices, letters, posters, newsletters or show schedules.

Some of the things that can go wrong are:

• Accidental mis-keying, as mentioned earlier.

• Deliberate sabotage of your data by aggrieved staff, computer hackers, etc.

• A temptation to waste a phenomenal amount of time – either your own or your staffs' – playing computer games.

• Probably worst of all, creating a false picture of the future business prospects. It is so easy to create wonderful forecasts that it is also easy to forget that 'the map is not the territory'. The computer can create these 'maps', but it can't force the paying customers to comply with them!

To summarise, while I'm not saying that a yard should not have a computer, I am saying that they are not the easy answer to office work that you may have been led to believe. If you do get one, make sure that:

• Everyone who is allowed to use it knows what they are doing.

• People who aren't authorised to use it can't get at it. This includes visiting children.

• All essential and confidential information is protected by passwords.

• You, or someone else, regularly backs-up (copies) everything onto floppy disks which are kept in a safe place away from the computer itself.

• You install anti-virus software.

Whatever method you use to do the paperwork, you should do it on a regular basis. Even the smallest yard will generate enough paper to take an hour a week, and it is best to do it at the same time each week. That way, you will develop a routine and it will get done, rather than being put off and put off until the VAT inspector arrives to make your life miserable, or the feed merchant refuses to supply you because you haven't paid the bills. If you really hate paperwork, get someone else to do it for you. There are plenty of freelances who will come to your place and do it all for you, including writing cheques so that you just have to sign them, checking bank statements, writing up the cash book and maintaining the horses' records.

There is no point in setting up elaborate administration systems if no one is prepared to maintain them. For instance, a big filing cabinet full of neatly labelled folders is lovely, but only if every piece of paper is in its proper folder. If it is sitting with a hundred other pieces of paper in a pile because you can't find the time to file them, you might just as well do without the filing cabinet.

For most purposes, a wallchart year planner and an enormous day-to-a-page diary will cover your needs. With a supply of paper-clips, you attach loose pieces of paper to the appropriate page of the diary – today's page for things you've dealt with today, or the relevant future day when you have to deal with them. That really *is* easy to do, and more to the point, it isn't too much of a distraction from what you really want to do out there with the horses.

11

Client Amenities and Public Relations

In order to succeed, any business not only has to provide what its customers need; it also has to ensure that potential customers know it can meet their needs better than the opposition. This gives us two points to consider – amenities and public relations.

The Riding Arena

Riding schools have a greater number of customers than pure livery yards, and these customers represent a greater cross-section of humanity than livery clients. You can be a bit picky about the latter, but not about pupils, or you just won't survive. To give lessons, you will need decent facilities which are not dependent on the weather or the state of the light, and this means a properly constructed and illuminated schooling area. Schools in the south of the country, where the weather is less severe, may be able to cope with an outdoor manège – provided it is properly constructed and surfaced.

What this will cost you obviously depends on what you have built, but you can expect, as a minimum, to pay a five-figure sum for a basic outdoor working area which is big enough to use as a dressage arena.

For teaching, especially novices, it is best if the arena is completely enclosed up to a height of 4ft (1.2m). Then, advantage-taking horses will not be able to leave the arena, and riders whose attention is elsewhere will not catch their feet on posts.

The most important factor – and this cannot be stressed too strongly – is site preparation and drainage. Skimp on this, especially if you have clay soil, and you will have constant problems with a manège that is unusable after rain. The site will need to be excavated to a depth – probably about 18in (45cm) – which allows the final work surface to be at ground level. Actual drainpipes may be needed, and over them a layer of brickbats and then one of coarse stones. This must be rolled level, and then the actual working surface can be laid on top. Three layers of 6in (15cm) of wood chips, interspersed with two layers of 2in (5cm) of sharp sand gives a good surface for most purposes; or pulverised bark or rubber shreds (rubbits) are a bit springier. Some salt may be needed to prevent surface-freezing in winter, and to avoid a layer of snow on top. American manège users, who have much greater extremes of weather to contend with than Britain, swear by salt as a method of keeping the surface damp. The theory is that the salt attracts the moisture in the air, and thus prevents the other material from drying out to dust. Some Americans also spread a layer of old sump oil to prevent dust, and say that it does not clog up on horses' feet.

All the surfaces mentioned are equally suitable for indoor schools, but the problems of dust are intensified, and so some system of sprinkling must be organised. All surfaces must be regularly raked or levelled. Harrowing tends to bring stones up to the surface, so the preferred method is to drag an old sleeper round behind a tractor.

In a rainy climate like ours, it is far preferable to have an indoor school, and then nothing stops the lessons – or your income. If you do not already have one, then you have the expensive problem of building, which usually means a loan. If your bank manager won't co-operate, your chosen construction company may be able to recommend a helpful finance house. They will not give you HP facilities themselves!

Write to several construction companies for estimates, and ask whether they will organise planning permission for you. This is rather specialised, and the average architect may not be the best person to obtain permission. There are a few freelances who specialise in indoor schools, and you may prefer to use one of those rather than feel tied by a construction company to using theirs. Ask the BHS or ABRS for help in selecting one. In general, it is not a good idea to do this sort of thing yourself, as there are many wrinkles involved which only experience can sort out. Remember that when you quote sizes to the contractors, they are going to interpret them as outside dimensions, so stress that the measurements you are quoting are internal. Continue to point this out to them at all stages, including the stage where the team arrives to start work. Better to be a nuisance than end up with a school smaller than you expected!

Go for a minimum height at the eaves of 16ft (5m), which will give you plenty of room for jumping, even with a foot (30cm) of surface on the floor. If you cannot afford a big school, go for a short, wide one, for it can easily be lengthened later, but not widened unless you are prepared to put up with columns in the middle. Width or 'span' usually goes up in set multiples. I am told that while steel and concrete prices are about the same for small spans, concrete for spans over 65ft (20m) costs a lot more, and is not really suitable as it needs to be much bulkier for adequate strength.

Allow at least three months for obtaining planning permission, and one month for construction. Your building will have to conform to British Standards specifications, which now include considerations of the length and density of human occupancy, and it will have to be passed by the Building Inspector at various stages during its construction before work can continue. The inspector will insist on proper drainage for the rainwater from the roof, and you may have to construct a soakaway for this some distance from the building. Despite the high initial cost involved, it might be worth installing a collection tank and pump system for sprinkling the school, or irrigating the fields, instead of paying high water rates for ever after.

If your site slopes, and you have to 'cut and fill' to level it, the council may insist on a *very* long wait for the fill to consolidate (even five years, maybe). Alternatively, the columns on the lower side will have to be longer and anchored at the original ground level.

You should have at least 25 per cent of translucent lights in the roof, and you can have some in the sides – but, in this case, beware of uneven light distribution on the floor. The council may insist on coloured roofing material (in preference to a coat of paint, which is more difficult to enforce) and this will add to delivery time. The council is not concerned with kicking boards. Railway sleepers used to be popular for this purpose, but they are now difficult to obtain and expensive, so marine ply is the usual alternative.

The price the construction company quotes will not include doors, gallery (unless specifically requested), kicking boards, sprinklers or lights, and they may not even wish to be involved in installing electric lights. These can be spotlights or strip lights, but the latter must be carefully situated to avoid a 'patchwork' effect. You can economise on doors by using a gate instead, but remember that you will need a fire exit as well as a main one, and that both should be wide enough and high enough for a horse and rider.

Galleries and judges' boxes will add a lot to the cost unless they are at ground level, although site excavation soil could be used to build them up. Most people will tolerate wooden benches to sit on, or you may be able to get seats from an old cinema. Whichever you choose, make sure they are high enough to allow occupants to see over the partition.

A public address system is useful, especially if you intend to hold shows or lecture/demonstrations. So is somewhere to plug in a music machine, or a heater in winter.

The normal procedure is to start with a basic building and add refinements later as you can afford them. The real benefit is a dry, lighted place to work in all year round, and you will certainly find that both pupils and livery clients will appreciate it and be prepared to pay a little more for it.

Facilities and Human Comforts

There are other refinements you can add to your premises which will also be appreciated. Decent parking space (without muddy puddles) for cars is almost essential. Wading through mud, getting dirty boots and splashed clothes are annoying to horsy people, but will cause even stronger feelings in unsuspecting parents. You may think Mama is silly to wear high-heeled sandals when she brings her child to ride, but she does not, and she is the one who chooses where the child rides. She will also appreciate a cosy waiting room or gallery from where she can watch the proceedings, and might also like the chance of a cup of coffee while she waits. Her child and other clients will also be glad of a drink after a hot lesson or a cold hack, so it might be worth installing a vending machine.

Decent toilets with hot water, a mirror and room to change are essential, despite the problem of who has to clean them. But they have got to be clean – nasty ones may be the deciding factor in the decision to go elsewhere!

Somewhere close to these facilities should be a pay phone, a notice board, first aid equipment and a boot cleaner. A map of where riding is permitted locally would do no harm, and you should, incidentally, be prepared to fight for hacking facilities in your area. If you take the trouble to be nice to the local farmers, they may even allow you to ride on their land, provided that no one lets out the stock or tramples the crops. They are more likely to be on your side if you buy feed and straw from them, and they may be able to let you have some extra grazing, or lend you some cattle to even up your own.

Public Relations

Good public relations consist of publicity and persuasion. Publicity means providing information of your existence, excellence, facilities and prices. Unless you are operating on a very large scale, or even on a specialised basis, advertising regularly can prove expensive in relation to the benefits it brings. It is better to keep your name in the local paper, or on the local radio, by providing them with information on any special activities you are planning, or any special achievements by your clients and staff. Make the most of your free entry in the telephone directory, and make sure the local libraries and Tourist Information Centres know of your existence.

The best and cheapest method of persuading new clients to come to you is that of personal recommendation by satisfied customers. The worst publicity, and quickest to spread, comes in the form of horror stories told by dissatisfied customers, and other local people you've upset.

The people who live near your yard may not like horses, and they will hate you if hoofprints appear on their lawns or grass verges, or if escapees are found eating their prize roses. They probably won't be too keen on having their children or pets trampled on, either, and they will make sure all their friends and acquaintances hear about it.

I find it difficult to comprehend the number of stable owners who snarl at strangers, even before they've found out what they want. If they are there to make trouble, it will be all the worse if you've antagonised them, and with any luck, you may be able to sweet-talk them out of it. They may be potential customers, or merely lost passers-by who know a potential customer, and if you help them they will tell their friends how nice you were. Whatever their status, they will certainly spread the word about their reception from you, be it good or bad.

In this country, unlike many others, the offended or neglected customer rarely makes a fuss, or demands value for money – she just goes away, never to come back again, and tells all her acquaintances how awful you were. Yet so often I've seen stable owners who are rude to their customers – even to livery owners who provide a steady income all year round! They either ignore them, fail to respond to their problems, or just don't make that little extra effort to make them feel wanted. How much effort does it cost you to smile, to greet people by name and ask how they are today? Too much? Then you are a churlish fool, and I hope you enjoy your bankruptcy.

Customers (even if you do not upset them) are notoriously fickle creatures, always seeking a bargain. If they do not consider you are giving them value for money, they'll look for it elsewhere; and short of pulling your socks up, there is nothing you can do about it. It is therefore pointless to be on bad terms with your local competitors on the grounds that they are stealing your customers. Bad-mouthing them will only get you a reputation for being bitchy, and it is also a waste of breath, for your audience will put it down to sour grapes. What you should be doing is getting together and seeing if you can't do each other some good. Your aims should be the same – that of encouraging the public to turn into horse people. Who wants to be a horse person when their reputation is of squabbling and backbiting?

The point is that any business operates in a community. With a business such as yours, it is most likely to be a rural community where communications are verbal but rapid, and where everyone likes to know what everybody else is doing. This is not nosiness, it is a genuine interest in one's neighbours, which will manifest itself by rallying round in times of trouble. A community is a collection of people, and if you will only play your part with other people it will be a happy community, providing lots of customers to make your business a success.

12

Making Extra Money

Whatever sort of stables you run, there is bound to come a time when you realise that the full financial potential of the place in its existing capacity has been reached. Financial expansion can only take place if some additional activities are started, so you begin to look around for something else to put a little jam on your bread and butter.

Further Uses of Amenities

If you are running a pure livery yard, the first thing that will come to mind is lessons for your clients. This tends to be a weekend activity unless you have an indoor school, but it is usually best done on an organised basis. If you do not wish, or feel competent, to do this teaching yourself, it might be worthwhile arranging for a freelance to do it, with your involvement being no more than a little cream off the top of her fee. The same consideration applies if you want to fly a little higher and get a 'name' to do some advanced clinics. It is usual with these to charge a small fee to spectators, and you really need a proper indoor school with seating facilities for this sort of enterprise.

Assuming that you have such a school, you could then go on to organise lecture/demonstrations by all sorts of people. But there is a snag – if you are not a riding school with public liability insurance, you will need to get some, for you will be inviting the general public onto your premises. Quite apart from that, you will need more car parking and toilet facilities, but you do have an opportunity to make a little extra by providing refreshments.

There is a whole series of non-horsy activities for which you can hire out your indoor school. Dog training, archery and barn dances are just a few possibilities, but you will have to be prepared to enforce the 'No Smoking' rule.

If you have invested in the video equipment I mentioned earlier, you can also use that for non-horsy activities, both on and off your premises. Members of the local golf and tennis clubs may be glad of the opportunity to observe their techniques, as may the archers I mentioned above. And of course, outside members of the local horse fraternity will be interested in the opportunity to see themselves on video.

Many riding schools boost their income in the school holidays by providing week-long courses for groups of foreign students, girl guides, etc., or by doing a series of stable management classes. You don't need an indoor school for the latter, but a lecture room would be useful, and this would also allow you to show films. Perhaps the local riding club might like to hire that room for the same sort of purpose, or for their regular meetings.

In the summer, many organisations will be holding fêtes, and they may like to include pony rides in their programmes. This obviously needs even-tempered animals, and a lot of helpers, for each pony will need a leader and a putter-upper. This sort of sideline may be beneath the dignity of larger schools, but smaller establishments could find it a useful way of boosting their income and getting themselves some new pupils. You either hire the ponies to the fête for the day, taking a percentage of their earnings, or you pay the fête for the 'pitch' and keep all the takings yourself. Either way, make sure your insurance company knows about it and that your public liability cover is adequate.

Selling Tack and Feed

If you have a room to spare, you may consider running a small shop. A stock of whips, hats and books wouldn't take too much capital, and if you have a little extra cash, you might like to add some more stock such as clothing and tack. (This issue is discussed in detail in *Running a Tack Shop as a Business*, Janet Macdonald, J.A. Allen 1986.) Once it becomes known that you keep such things, clients will ask you to get them anything you don't have in stock. If you can't come to some mutually advantageous arrangement with your local tack shop on such matters, then you are no business person!

On the subject of selling things, why not sell feed? Proper feed merchants tend to be few and far between, and horse owners with a field and a small shed are quite common, especially those with limited storage space. The average feed merchant can't be bothered with delivering small quantities, so the hapless owner has to go and collect her own feed. If you are closer, she is likely to come to you instead. The volume of such sales may not be large, but may well be enough to enable you to buy your own supplies in bulk, which means more cheaply, so you have two chances of winning. If you decide to do this, it might be sensible to restrict what you sell to the feedstuffs you use yourself, as this will mean you don't have feed going stale before it is sold.

Breeding, Breaking and Dealing – a Caution

BREEDING

It is a common assumption that extra cash can be made by breeding. If a livery owner is involved in this, perhaps with a lame mare, it will not be too bad, as they will be paying for the extra care and feeding involved. But unless you have plenty of space it is not such a good idea, for the mare and new-born foal will need a paddock to themselves, or the mare may attack any curious horses. Another hazard is aggrieved livery owners whose horses have not been turned out because the mare and foal were in the only field.

Breeding from your own stock on a small scale is not financially advantageous either, partly for the reasons which I will explain shortly, but mainly because of the sheer cost of breeding and raising youngsters, and their relatively low value at the end of it all. And it takes so long to get a return. Even professional breeders make little on their youngstock unless they are of outstanding show quality. The same applies to keeping a stallion at stud. Unless he is a show winner, he just isn't going to earn his keep, so forget it. I'm not talking here of your own personal riding horses, which you will be keeping anyway, but of animals acquired specifically for this purpose, or retained when they are of no other use to you. Breeding and showing to win and make money is no game for beginners.

BREAKING AND SCHOOLING

Breaking and/or schooling other people's animals is another possible way of achieving extra earnings, but it does require a high degree of expertise in both riding and horse handling. (The mere horse psychology takes experience to apply, for no two spoilt horses are alike.) Until you have a reputation for this, all you are going to get is other peoples' problems, which will be time-consuming and probably not all that lucrative. Also, since the problems will most likely have been caused by the owner, they will recur as soon as the horse goes back home, and the owner will conclude that you didn't do much of a job!

DEALING

Most establishments do a little buying and selling, which usually seems like a good idea at first. They reason that all you need is the ability to pick a good horse at the right price, and to persuade someone to buy him fairly rapidly at a better price. Thereby hangs the inevitable snag. If you don't sell him rapidly, you've got to keep him, and that costs money. That's obvious, I know, but what many people do not realise is exactly what it *does* cost. Not just the feed, and maybe a set of shoes: it costs exactly what a livery would have paid for the use of the box the sale horse occupies, plus the effort you have to put into looking after him.

It is easy to buy a horse for £2,000, sell him ten weeks later for £2,600, take off a bit for feed and shoes (let's say £250) and tell yourself how clever you were to make £350 on him. But let's set that out and see what it should really look like:

	£
Cost of horse	£2,000
2 sets of shoes	100
Advert in *Horse and Hound*	20
Ten weeks lost livery @ £100 per week	1,000
TOTAL COST	3,120
Income from sale	2,600
Loss on sale	520
Loss of interest on capital*	15
TOTAL LOSS	£535

* (ten weeks deposit interest at 4% per annum)

Do the same thing a month later, and you'll be even more out of pocket, especially if the box has stood empty in between. Moral – a little dealing is a good thing if you can't get enough liveries to fill your boxes, but if you can, you should be a bit more careful when fixing your selling prices.

Running Shows

The final thought that comes to mind on making extra money is to run some shows. If you have an indoor school, you could hold indoor jumping or indoor dressage shows all winter, but the best bet is outdoor events. Combined training, hunter trials and actual shows are all popular with the horsy fraternity, although the neighbours might get annoyed if you do it too often. As long as you don't overdo it, or cause noise or traffic problems, you may not need planning permission for shows.

In view of the many epidemics of equine diseases (coughs,

ringworm, etc.) you would probably be wise to keep outside competitors and their horses out of your actual yard and home paddocks. You cannot prevent your own clients' horses meeting others away from home, but there is no harm in minimising risks. For this reason, the furthest field you have is best, with drinking water, toilets and first aid laid on, so no one has to go to your yard. You should also consider having the show field harrowed before you graze your own stock on it again, to break up the potentially worm-infested droppings of strange horses.

You can hire all the equipment you need, from ring-ropes to toilets. Look through the show editions of *Horse and Hound* (published in March) for useful addresses, or get a copy of the *Showman's Directory*.

Be warned, however. Don't jump in at the deep end or you may catch cold. All the people I know who have run shows emphasise the wisdom of starting small. On a small scale, it is fairly easy to enlist friends and acquaintances as stewards and course builders/repairers. You won't need to hire many jumps or an elaborate public address system (if you need one at all). You will be able to use fairly local people to judge instead of having to go to the official lists, and judges' expenses will be less. Competitors will not look down their noses at photocopied schedules, and they will not expect vast prize money or grandiose trophies. Incidentally, the wise show organiser awards challenge trophies. They may be a bore to recover each year, but they don't have to be replaced, so they are cheaper in the long run.

If you aim for a friendly yet efficient atmosphere, people will be keen to come back again, and they will pass the word around among their friends. You will be able to have several of these small shows in a season, making a little money from each one, and so long as you keep your cool in difficult situations, everyone will go away happy. And you should be equally happy as you go to bank your takings!

Appendix 1 - *Cash Book (Income)*

		Detail	Income	Bank	Livery	Lessons	Other
March	2	Cash	150			150	
		Smith	400		400		
		Jones	400		400		
March	3	Cash	180			180	
		Green	280		280		
		Mason	400		400		
March	4	Cash	165			165	
March	5	Cash	210			210	
				2,185			
March	6	Cash	210			210	
		Black	280		280		
		Shepherd	400		400		
		Weston	400		400		
		Broom	280		280		
March	7	Cash	195			195	
		Warren	400		400		
		Richards	280		280		
				2,445			
March	9	Cash	195			195	
March	10	Cash	210			210	
March	11	Cash	210			240	
March	12	Cash	240			240	
March	13	Cash	615			615	
March	14	Cash	585			585	
				2,085			Manure
March	16	Cash	200			180	20
March	17	Cash	180			180	
March	18	Cash	165			165	
March	19	Cash	270			270	
March	20	Cash	630			630	
March	21	Cash	570			570	
				2,015			
March	23	Cash	165			165	
March	24	Cash	165			165	
March	25	Cash	210			210	Lecture/ demo
March	26	Cash	615			150	465
March	27	Cash	645			645	
March	28	Cash	585			585	
				2,385			
March	30	Cash	165			165	
March	31	Cash	180			180	
				345			
			11,460	11,460	3,520	7,455	485

(VAT proportion = £114.60

Appendix 1 – *Cash Book (Expenditure)*

			Chq. No.	Amount	Wages & Staff	Free-lance	Feed
Mar.	5	Petty Cash	641	100			
		S. E. Insurance Brokers	642	396			
		Borough Bromley	643	675.50	675.50		
		British Telecom	644	156.68			
	12	Swanson	645	225.00			
		Western Roofing Co	646		460.00		
		Village Saddler	647	47.80			
	19	Jackson Smyth	648	136.00			
		Patullo Higgs	649	2100.00		210.00	
		Smith Garage	650	166.56			
	26	Mrs George	651	400.00		400.00	
		Cash	652	576.00	576.00		
		Inland Revenue	653	224.00	224.00		
		Swanson	654	180.00			
		Patel (Grocer)	655	249.14	249.14		
				6092.68	1049.14	400.00	2100.00

98

Vet Farrier	Tack	Petty Cash	Motor	VAT		Other
		100.00				
			396			
					Rates	675.50
				23.44	Phone	133.24
	191.49		33.51			
				68.51	Roofs	391.49
		40.68		7.12		
115.74				20.26		
			140.90	25.66		
	153.19			28.81		
115.74	394.68	40.68	100.00	536.90	205.31	1200.23

Appendix 2 - *Petty Cash Book*

			Bank	Other	Total/In
Mar.	5	Cheque No 641	100.00		100.00
	12	Manure 3 Bags		3.00	3.00
	24	Manure 2 Bags		2.00	2.00
	27	Manure 3 Bags		4.00	4.00
		Manure 3 Bags		3.00	3.00
		22 Bales Straw		4.00	4.00
	30	Manure 8 Bags		8.00	8.00
		1 Bale Hay		3.00	3.00
	31	Manure 3 Bags		3.00	3.00
		Manure 4 Bags		4.00	4.00
		2 Bales Straw		4.00	4.00
		12 lb Corn		4.80	4.80

142.80

				Horse	Domestic	Other	VAT
Mar.	Balance	b/fwd	4.48				
	2	Village Saddlery	5.88	5.00			.88
		Coffee, Sugar	4.84		4.84		
	9	Elastoplast	1.80			1.80	
		Stamps	8.00			8.00	
	16	Coffee, Sugar etc.	6.49		6.49		
		Envelopes	1.20			1.20	
		Milk	6.93		6.93		
		Dustmen	5.00			5.00	
	31	Coffee, Sugar	4.84		4.84		
		Milk	6.93		6.93		
		Stamps	2.60			2.60	
		Balance fwd	83.81				
			142.80				

Appendix 3 - *Cash Flow Forecast*

	Jan		Feb		Mar		Apl	
	Actual	Budget	Actual	Budget	Actual	Budget	Actual	Budget
Income								
Livery (5 horses)	2000	2000	2000	2000	2000	2000		2100
Half livery (5 horses)	1500	1500	1500	1500	1500	1500		1600
Lessons (10 horses)	6630	7200	6885	7200	7050	7200		7200
Shows/demos					465	400		
Manure sales		50	37	50	65	50		50
Total Income	10130	10750	10422	10750	11080	11150		10950
Expenditure								
Loan repayments	5550	5550						
Rates					2000	2000		
Insurance			2678	2800				
Electricity	1542	1600						1600
Motor expenses	322	400	482	400	284	400		400
Staff costs	796	800	796	800	796	800		900
Freelance costs	380	400	440	400	380	400		450
Telephone	157	180						200
Repairs & maint. yard		150		150	460	150		150
Repairs & maint. field								
Feed	2550	2700	2469	2700	2230	2700		2200
Hay/straw/chips	100	100	100	100	120	100		100
Vet	36	80		80	228	160		80
Farrier	480	500	460	500	530	500		500
Tack, new & repairs	156	200	34	200		200		200
General	45	50	36	50	22	50		50
Contingencies						250		
VAT			4678	5000				
Total Expenditure	12114	12710	12173	13180	7050	7710		6830
Month's balance	(1984)	(1960)	(1751)	(2430)	4030	3440		4120
Cumulative balance	(1984)	(1960)	(3735)	(4390)	295	(950)		3170

May		Jun		Jul Aug Sep	Oct Nov Dec	Jan Feb Mar	Apl May Jun	Jul Aug Sep	Oct Nov Dec
Actual	Budget	Actual	Budget	Budget	Budget	Budget	Budget	Budget	Budget
	2100		2100	6300	6300	6300	6600	6600	6600
	1600		1600	4800	4800	4800	5100	5100	5100
	7200		7200	21600	23000	23000	23000	23000	24200
			2000	2000	400	400	2500	2500	500
	50		50	150	150	150	150	150	150
	10950		12950	34850	34650	34650	37350	37350	36550
				5550		5550		5550	
				800		800		800	
						2400			
				1500	1700	1900	1600	1600	1800
	400		400	1200	2000	1200	1200	1200	2200
	900		900	2700	2700	2700	3000	3000	3000
	450		450	1400	1400	1400	1400	1500	1500
				200	200	200	200	200	200
	150		150	500	500	500	500	500	500
				400			1000	500	
	2000		2000	6000	7500	7000	6000	6000	8000
	100		7500	2300	300	3000	8000	2500	300
	80		80	300	300	400	300	300	300
	500		500	1600	1600	1600	1600	1800	1800
	200		200	600	600	600	600	600	600
	50		50	150	150	150	150	150	150
			250	750	750	750	750	750	750
	5000			5000	5000	6000	6000	6000	6000
	9830		12480	30950	24700	36150	32300	32950	27100
	1120		470	3900	9950	(1500)	5050	4400	9450
	4290		4760	8660	18610	17110	22160	26560	36010

Appendix 4 – *Record Card*

OSCAR
Foaled 1988 Bought 4/92 £2260
Basic Ration: 6 Oats 3 Nuts 2 Bran 14 Hay

1997	Feed Variations	Hours Worked	Shoes	Tack	Veterinary	Other
Jan		66	4	Lead Rope £5		Trace clip
Feb		60	4			
Mar		64	4		Wormed £8	
Apr	7 days no oats				Colic £42	Insurance
	7 days 2 oats	38	4			
May	Out at night					
	no hay	65	4	Headcollar		
Jun	3 days no oats			repair £12		
	3 days 14 hay				Cut leg –	
	rest out, no hay	55	4		minor, no vet.	
July	No hay	67	4		Boosters –	
					anti-tet,	
					'flu, teeth rasp	
					general check	
					£88	
August				2 Brushes £8.50		

Appendix 5 - Useful Addresses

British Horse Society,
British Equestrian Centre,
Kenilworth,
Warks. CV8 2LR

Association of British Riding Schools,
Queens Chambers, 38–40 Queen Street,
Penzance,
Cornwall TR18 4BH

Manpower Services Commission,
New Enterprises Programme,
Elisabeth House, 16 St Peter's Square,
Manchester M2 3DF

HM Customs & Excise, VAT Central Unit,
Alexander House, 21 Victoria Avenue,
Southend-on-Sea SS99 1AA

Showman's Directory,
Lance Publications,
45 Bridge Street,
Godalming GU7 1HL

Independent Financial Advisers
For a list of licensed financial advisers in your area, contact the
Personal Investment Association (PIA),
1 Canada Square,
London E14 5AZ

Appendix 6 – *Tax-deductible Expenses*

Any sums expended wholly and exclusively for the purposes of the business may usually be deducted in the computation of profits. These sums must be of a 'day-to-day' nature, and not for capital items such as horses, buildings, or purchased vehicles (lease charges for leased vehicles may be claimed). This list is intended to be a guide, and is not exhaustive. Always obtain receipts for expenditure, and keep these for your accountant to check.

- Advertising
- Loan interest
- Insurance premiums
- Redundancy payments
- Wages, pensions and employer's National Insurance contributions
- Bad debts
- Legal expenses not connected with capital items
- Rent and rates
- Repair and maintenance charges
- Hire charges on vehicles or machinery
- Subscriptions to societies and periodicals
- Other business expenditure: telephone; light and heat; postage and stationery; staff refreshments; furniture for staff rooms, waiting rooms and offices; specialist working clothes for staff and proprietor (boots, breeches, uniforms, etc.); all expenditure on horses' feed, clothing and care (tack may be treated as capital items); feed for guard dog; specialised teaching equipment.

Index